Caribbean Contract with Her Boss

—

Nina Singh

Recycling programs
for this product may
not exist in your area.

ISBN-13: 978-1-335-73697-0

Caribbean Contract with Her Boss

Copyright © 2023 by Nilay Nina Singh

For questions and comments about the quality of this book, please contact us at CustomerService@Harlequin.com.

Harlequin Enterprises ULC
22 Adelaide St. West, 41st Floor
Toronto, Ontario M5H 4E3, Canada
www.Harlequin.com

Printed in U.S.A.

Nina Singh lives just outside Boston, Massachusetts, with her husband, children and a very rambunctious Yorkie. After several years in the corporate world, she finally followed the advice of family and friends to "give the writing a go, already." She's oh-so-happy she did. When not at her keyboard, she likes to spend time on the tennis court or golf course. Or immersed in a good read.

Books by Nina Singh

Harlequin Romance

How to Make a Wedding

From Tropical Fling to Forever

Destination Brides

Swept Away by the Venetian Millionaire

Their Festive Island Escape
Her Billionaire Protector
Spanish Tycoon's Convenient Bride
Her Inconvenient Christmas Reunion
From Wedding Fling to Baby Surprise
Around the World with the Millionaire
Whisked into the Billionaire's World
Wearing His Ring till Christmas

Visit the Author Profile page at Harlequin.com.

To Becks, for being more loving and loyal than I could have ever imagined.

CHAPTER ONE

RAFAEL MALTA SIGNED off on the final document and closed the file on his laptop. That was it. Everything was settled, all the *i*'s dotted and all the *t*'s crossed. He'd left no detail unattended. His life here in Seattle was essentially over.

Good riddance.

And not a moment too soon. He wouldn't miss it in the least. And he certainly had no plans to look back.

His last brief relationship had gone sour. Really sour. Rafe blew out an ironic laugh. That was one way to put it. Trina had said all the right things when everything had begun, but in the end, she'd walked. She hadn't been able to stand by him through the turmoil.

No, there was nothing left for him here. He'd never really had many friends in the city to begin with. Nothing remained but painful memories, sharp anger and hurtful loss. It was beyond time to make a clean break.

And make a clean break he would.

By this time tomorrow he'd be deplaning on Puerto Rican soil in San Juan. His titles of developer and investor would be wiped off his profile. Now those monikers would have the disclaimer *former* in front of them. His new official title, as of about 9:00 a.m. this morning, included the words "Owner/Operator, Gato Rum Distillery." And if he was a novice at this next endeavor he was embarking on, well, so be it. There had to be a reason this opportunity had randomly fallen in his lap. Besides, he considered himself a fast learner, especially when he was highly motivated to achieve a particular goal. And this goal had him really, really motivated. He couldn't fail. There was no plan B at this stage in his life. He'd used up all his second chance cards.

This next stage of his life would be much more than a business venture. It was an adventure—a whole new way of life. His goal was to become a completely different person. He'd shed the ghosts of his previous life.

A brief knock on the door pulled him out of his thoughts. A moment later, his administrative assistant walked in. He'd employed Patty since he'd started his businesses many years ago. She was the only person who had stuck by him throughout the scandals and accusations.

She held up a yellow folder full of paperwork. "Look what you've done."

Rafe had no idea what she might be referring to. He knew for a fact he hadn't overlooked anything as far as her severance and retirement package were concerned.

"Are you sure you won't want to come with me after all?" he asked rhetorically. They'd been over this before. "The offer still stands, you know."

Patty walked farther into the room and held the folder to her chest. "My dear Rafe, if only I was a couple of decades younger and hadn't become a devoted grandmother of four yet. I would take you up on your generous offer in a heartbeat. But alas, I'm old and I'm tired."

"You're not that old, Patty. And you have more energy than most of the newly graduated college students I've employed over the years."

She sighed with a small smile. "I'm old and tired enough, Rafe. With this project, I'm afraid you're on your own."

Rafe had to scoff at that. Nothing new there. He'd been on his own for quite some time now, even while he'd still had a living parent.

Now there was no one. And that suited him just fine.

Patty continued, "But I might take you up on the offer to come visit at some point. I've never been to Puerto Rico. It sounds like paradise."

He was counting on it. "Anytime. On me. I'll arrange for your flight and you can stay at the hacienda that houses the distillery. Just say when."

"You have yourself a deal, Mr. Malta."

"That includes Frank and the grandkids, by the way."

Her smile widened. "You're too generous." A mist appeared over her eyes. "I'm going to miss you, Rafe."

Rafe could only nod. He appreciated the words—he really did. But in the end, they were just words. Patty was one of the most loyal and genuine people he'd ever met. In fact, she'd grown close to serving as a mother figure in Rafe's life. No doubt she meant what she said. But he wasn't naive—she'd eventually stop thinking about Rafe altogether. Her employment at Malta Enterprises would just be a fond memory. She may visit once or twice but in due time, the visits would stop, too. Everyone eventually moved on. It was just the way of the world.

"Promise you'll take care of yourself." Patty's voice hitched.

Dear heavens, was she about to cry? Despite himself, a lump of emotion settled at the base of his throat. Patty had been the only person who had genuinely expressed concern for him during the hell on earth that was the past year. She had been the only one to listen to his side of things, ignoring the salacious gossip about the physical altercation he'd been involved in at a swanky nightclub that fateful night—a night that had turned his entire life upside down.

Apparently, she'd been more worried about him than he'd realized or acknowledged.

Rafe stood up from his desk and moved to where the woman stood. He couldn't recall the last time he'd so much as touched her, but the moment appeared to call for a hug of some sort.

"I'll miss you too, Patty," he said past the unfamiliar lump in his throat and limply looped his arms around her shoulders. Her response was to wrap her arms tight around his midsection and hiccup against his chest.

Rafe felt disoriented. Of course, he'd had women cry in his arms before. But those occurrences had been the result of broken relationships, the aftermath of romantic entanglements having run their course. What was happening now, this true display of emotion, was unfamiliar to say the least. This felt raw and exposed. As much as he appreciated Patty's affection for him, he didn't know quite what to say or do.

So he did all he could think of. He just returned her hug.

* * *

The new boss needs to see you.

Eva bit back the curse on her tongue at the text from her brother that greeted her first thing in the morning. The man he referred to was not her boss. He was the reason her whole life had just been upturned.

Well, not the sole reason. She bore plenty of responsibility for that turn of events herself. Now everyone she loved would have to pay for her mistakes. Eva squeezed her eyes shut against the pain. She'd make it up to them all if it was the last thing she did.

Her phone pinged again.

Get down here, already. He's waiting for you.

Eva couldn't help the bristle that ran through her body at that thought.

Who was she kidding? Technically he *was* her boss—for the next forty-eight hours at least. The purchase agreement said she had to stick around that long to show him around the operation and answer any questions he may have. Eva fervently wished Papá hadn't signed off on that part.

Not that she could blame her father one bit for any of this. Eva was the reason all this was happening. The loss of their family distillery. Their very home.

As far as she knew, this Rafael Malta was a technology entrepreneur who'd developed an application used around the world. The man didn't know a thing about distilling rum. How forty-eight hours was going to be enough time to get him situated was beyond her.

Well, it wasn't her problem any longer.

She scoffed. As if she really believed that.

What happened here would always concern her, even if she couldn't do anything about it anymore. Eva had to bite back the ever-ready sob that sat consistently at the back of her throat these days.

Gato Rums would always be a part of her. The place was in her genes, her very bones. Her ancestors had cultivated this land and distilled high quality product for close to a century. The hacienda and distillery... It was all part of her genetic makeup. And she'd destroyed that legacy.

The stinging behind her eyes grew to fully shed tears. Whatever it took, she would make this all up to her family somehow. She had to. Or she wouldn't be able to live with herself.

It was past time for any kind of despair or wallowing. She had a goal and she'd do whatever it took to achieve it. Regardless of the obstacles, she'd rectify this mistake.

Not that she had any clue as to *how* at the moment.

Aside from the lack of resources, one inconvenient variable in the form of a tech billionaire immediately stood in her way. Rafe Malta didn't seem the type who would budge easily. So be it. Eva would simply have to move around him. In the meantime, she had to make do with the cards dealt to her. And for the next forty-eight hours, she had to play Rafe Malta's helpful assistant.

She could do this. She just had to stay strong and focus on the future, when she could finally try and fix her mess.

It really didn't help that the man was so good-looking: Tall with bronze, tanned skin and dark green eyes that could make a woman wallow in their depths. Dark hair that fell in waves over his forehead. Not that she had any way of knowing, but she got the impression he didn't wear his hair so casually all that often. Eva made a mental note to look him up online later. She'd done a cursory search, but her psyche hadn't been able to endure dwelling too much on the various personal details of the new owner of Gato Rums. She'd been much too focused on

how to rectify the calamities that had led to
Rafe Malta becoming owner in the first place.

Now, dressed in khakis and a crisp white silk
shirt, he seemed out of place on the dirt road
leading to the main house.

He was talking to Teo and seemed to be taking notes on a tablet. Eva couldn't help her audible scoff at that notion. Rum distilling and
distribution wasn't a process one learned by
taking notes.

She must have been louder than she'd intended as both men immediately looked up
and Rafe's gaze landed squarely on her face.
Teo gave a small nod in greeting. Her brother
seemed visibly relieved to see her. She couldn't
really blame him. Teo had never been terribly
invested in the family business. His interests
ran more along the lines of fast cars and the
international racing circuit. Eva and her father
were the real backbone of Gato Rum. Another
stab of guilt lanced her chest. Her brother's return to the distillery was supposed to have been
short-lived. But then everything had gone to
Hades.

All because Eva had trusted the wrong man.
She'd been foolish enough to fall in love with
him, even. She'd never believe in love again.

So it annoyed her that there was a tingle of

awareness traveling over her skin as Rafe Malta's gaze held steady on her.

Shut it all down.

After her disastrous sham of a marriage, she was done with men—especially the tall, dark and handsome types—for the foreseeable future. Maybe forever, in fact. Giving Victor any control over her family's estate and business had been the biggest mistake of her life. Her ex-husband had literally gambled it all away.

Her brother gave her a wave as she started making her way over the gravel path to where they stood. "Hey, sis, we've been waiting for you."

"Here I am."

Rafe extended his hand to her as she approached them. "Pleased to finally meet you, Ms. Gato."

Teo clapped him on the back of the shoulder in a familiar gesture, as if they'd been friends for decades. That was just Teo's nature, she knew. But she couldn't help the hint of irritation the action caused within her.

"No need to be so formal, my man," her brother said. "That's just Ev."

Whoa, just because Teo was already growing friendly with the man didn't mean *she* was anywhere near ready for that kind of cordiality.

She thrust her hand out to shake the one Rafe offered. "Evalyn."

Teo quirked an eyebrow at her with a hint of a smile on his lips. True, she never used her full name in any context. But it seemed appropriate to do so under the current circumstances.

"Nice to meet you," Rafe said again, still holding on to her hand. He had strong fingers, warm and roughened. Surprising, given that he was supposed to be a straitlaced, businessman who probably even had people to do his grocery shopping.

But as she studied him, Eva realized her mistake. This man wasn't soft in any way, shape or form. She'd be a fool to underestimate him. The awareness traveling over her skin intensified.

She tugged her hand out of his grasp.

Teo cleared his throat and made an exaggerated show of glancing at his watch. "I'll leave you two to it, then."

He was leaving? What the…?

"Where are you going?" she demanded to her brother's retreating back.

"I told Sam I'd cover the shop for him while he goes to an appointment. I think you can handle this on your own."

Ha! She wasn't as sure about that as Teo seemed to be.

Traitor. So tempting to yell the word out loud,

but Eva bit her tongue and watched silently as Teo jogged to his classic Mustang parked on the other side of the driveway.

She was on her own, then.

An awkward silence ensued, one Eva had no idea how to end. And Rafe didn't seem inclined to. He just stood there, smiling at her. Waiting for her to make the next move.

Which made sense, she supposed. She was the one in charge of getting the new owner accustomed to the estate, after all.

"Teo mentioned you had already begun a tour?" It was as good a start as any.

Rafe nodded. "A very general one. I was told you'd be the one to get me into all the finer details."

Eva toed one of the small pebbles at her feet. "Lucky me," she muttered in a barely audible tone.

"I beg your pardon?" Apparently the man had bat-sensitive hearing.

"Nothing. Never mind. Forget it."

He crossed his arms in front of his chest, his gaze fixed squarely on her face. "I'd rather not forget it. You clearly don't want to be here."

Wow. Straight to the point. No shirking the issue with this guy. Eva wasn't sure she liked that.

Besides, it wasn't the location that was the

issue. Under normal circumstances, Eva loved being here. She loved every inch of this property. This was her home. Well, it used to be.

"How perceptive of you." She couldn't help the mild taunt. If she was making him uncomfortable, well, that made two of them.

His only reaction was a slight quirk of an eyebrow. "Anything you'd like to get off your chest, Ms. Gato?"

Did she ever. But where would she even start?

"I'm not sure you'd understand, Mr. Malta."

He sighed and rubbed his forehead with a weariness that surprised her. What exactly was his story?

Not that she cared one way or another.

"Look," he began. "Why don't we at least start by dropping the formalities? Please call me Rafe. May I call you Evalyn?"

She nodded in silence and he continued.

"I haven't been here long enough to offend you. So why the animosity?"

Eva narrowed her eyes on his face as she tried to summon an appropriate answer. One thing she could say for him—he was pretty direct.

Maybe she needed to be as well.

The greenish-hazel eyes staring back at Rafe held an intensity that unnerved him, more so than any high-stakes negotiation or high-pressure client meeting he could recall. Something about this woman was throwing him off, making him second-guess himself and the words he chose.

How very uncharacteristic for him.

But there was more behind her eyes. A clear wound.

Whoever had put that hurt there must have been very important to her...at some point in time, anyway. Was he still?

Rafe gave his head a small shake. The answer to that question was none of his concern. He was here for one reason only: to begin his new life in his new field—that of rum distillery proprietor and operator. He couldn't be thinking of anything personal when it came to this woman.

In fact, he shouldn't have even asked her what he had. It really was none of his business why she seemed to have taken such a keen dislike to him. Something about his personality seemed to rub some folks the wrong way, as he'd found out at a young age. Even his mother had barely tolerated him.

He was used to it, after all. Just another person all too ready to think the worst of him, without so much as getting to know him in any way. He supposed at least this time said person had good reason. Somehow, that made it less personal. Less cutting.

Not that it mattered one way or another.

He watched as she chewed the inside of her cheek and examined him. He got the distinct impression she found him lacking based on what she saw. Just when he thought she was going to ignore his question, she finally spoke. "I have nothing against you personally."

That was something, at least. But she didn't give him a chance for any kind of victory celebration as she continued. "But your presence here does indeed offend me."

That was harsh. "Ouch. That sounds rather personal indeed."

She lifted an eyebrow. "It isn't. Just an observation. I don't think you're here for the right reasons. And I don't think you'll last here long."

She had no idea just how wrongly she'd pegged him. For all his faults, Rafe had never been a quitter. There hadn't been anyone there for him offering support or guidance throughout most of his life. So he'd made sure to find the drive within himself. And he'd succeeded.

Clearly, the woman before him was no quitter either. No doubt that was part of her resentment. Whereas Rafe had chosen to give up the life and career he'd built for himself, Eva was being forced to relinquish something she clearly still wanted and she obviously resented it. Apparently, she was set on taking that resentment out on him.

Not exactly the way he'd hoped to start this venture. But so be it. A challenge was simply an obstacle to overcome. He'd certainly had his share of those.

Eva was hardly the first to resent his presence. He hadn't been wanted as a child and he hadn't been wanted at the fancy, expensive boarding school he'd attended on a scholarship. No one had exactly befriended him at university either.

"What if you are underestimating me?" he asked Eva now, pulling his mind away from the useless memories.

She shrugged one elegant shoulder. "I don't think I am."

He would have to prove it to her. For some reason, despite having just met her mere moments ago, Eva Gato's impression of him mattered. In fact, he couldn't recall the last time he'd placed such importance on the opinion of another individual. Surprising, indeed.

"You sound like you don't give me much credit as a businessman."

She immediately shook her head. "No. You've clearly reached pinnacles of professional success. That's not the issue."

"What is?"

"Isn't it obvious? I have no faith in your ability to run a rum operation. You have no experience, no knowledge. This was clearly an impulse buy for you, the way someone might grab a pack of gum in the grocery store as they check out."

Rafe couldn't help but chuckle. She really didn't think much of him, did she?

"I put a bit more thought into it than that. A lot of research was gathered and analyzed."

"Sounds like you did some reading, huh?"

"You really think I'm going to fall flat on my face here, don't you? That I'm going to fail."

She remained silent, but the answer to his question was clear in her eyes. Suddenly, nothing in the world mattered as much to him as proving her wrong. And there was something else. Rafe realized he was actually enjoying himself. Verbally sparring with her was the most pleasure he'd experienced in weeks, if not months. "What if I told you I'll be able to turn this place around and have it earning a higher profit by next season?"

"I believe that's what you think."

He should be insulted, but instead he felt a hint of excitement at the challenge in her tone. "We could place a bet on it, even."

Eva's reaction was swift and wholly unexpected. Her jaw clenched, her eyebrows pulled together, her lips snapped tight. "I don't care much for gambling, Mr. Malta. Especially not about matters that involve the property and distillery that have been in my family for two generations."

She was back to calling him Mr. Malta and he could have sworn the temperature had just plummeted several degrees. Or maybe that was just the iciness in her tone.

What had he said? He couldn't seem to stop his missteps around this woman. "Of course. I only meant to suggest a simple, friendly wager."

She remained silent, her eyes still cold. Finally, she turned on her heel without so much as a preamble or any kind of acknowledgement of his apology. "Let's get started," she stated without sparing him another glance.

Rafe did the only thing he could. He silently followed her.

CHAPTER TWO

WHAT WAS IT about her that pulled such men into her orbit? Men who were so eager to recklessly gamble on things that meant nothing to them but meant the whole world to others. Men like her ex-husband. Not that Rafe would be around her for long. Thank heavens for that. There was something about the man that was unsettling her, rattling her nerves.

Even now, despite her irritation with him, his presence behind her had her off-balance. An awareness seemed to be sizzling between them.

She had to get a grip on it already. After the calamity that was her former marriage, she knew better than to feel any kind of pull toward any man, let alone this particular one.

As it was, this handoff process was tantamount to emotional torture. The sooner she got it over with, the better for her psyche.

"We'll start with the fermentation room." She threw the words over her shoulder as she led him around the pathway to the gray brick building behind it. "It's where we start the process. We begin with only four ingredients— raw sugarcane, fresh mountain water, unrefined yeast and unrefined molasses."

She led him through the large wooden doors and pointed to the large vat in the center of the room. "It's all fermented in here for about six days or so."

Rafe appeared to be studying his surroundings with interest and total focus. That was something, at least. "Got it," he said.

"After fermentation, we take the resulting wash and transfer it into sills."

He nodded once. "I recall reading about that."

Again with the reading.

"I beg your pardon?" he asked.

She hadn't meant to say it out loud, hadn't even realized she'd spoken the thought.

"Never mind," she answered.

But Rafe remained still where he stood. "No, please. Go ahead and speak your mind. I get the feeling you typically do. What is it that you're thinking at the moment?"

Fine. If that's what he wanted, she would oblige. "Simply that this isn't the kind of business you can learn from the pages of a book. It takes years of trial and error."

The corner of his mouth lifted. Was he smirking at her? Ire spiked in her chest.

"Luckily, you and your family have already taken care of that part," he said without an ounce of irony.

Eva's ire turned to flat-out fury. Did he think he was making some kind of valid point?

"Yes. We did. All so a billionaire could swoop in and take the reins because he became bored with his life."

The smirked widened. "You think I'm swooping, huh?"

Eva rubbed her forehead. This was useless. She was getting all worked up while he acted like this was just a big joke. Rafe was the type who clearly didn't understand that book smarts could only get a person so far in this business. Something told her he was going to find that out the hard way.

"Why don't we move on?" She turned on her heel and continued forward without waiting for a response. "Then the wash is heated until the alcohol separates. Then it's just a matter of aging it."

He paused before finally falling in step with her once more. "How long does that take?"

"We're very particular about our aging process so we take a bit longer than most other family-owned distilleries. At least two years. The aging is done in a different warehouse. We can head there next."

The rest of the morning went by in a blur. Eva did her best to relay information about the process as clearly and precisely as possible, and Rafe's expression toward the end told her he was beginning to finally realize what a massive project he'd taken on. Throughout the tour, she introduced him to the foreman and various other employees.

The resignation in her foreman's eyes had nearly broken her. The man had been with them since she was a teen. Now he'd found himself employed by a stranger from the States.

All thanks to her.

With a shake of her head, Eva forced herself to focus on the task at hand—getting through this tour.

She'd saved the best for last. "We can head to the tasting room to finish up," she told Rafe, leading him up the steel steps to the second floor, which housed the small kitchen and bar area. "It's run by an amazing chef, Francesca Riberi." There was no need to tell him that she and Francesca had been friends since college in Boston. Or that her family had hired Fran right after they'd both graduated, Fran with a hospitality degree and Eva with one in business management.

"Fran is a genius at creating bite-size crudités to accompany our rum tastings," Eva told Rafe. "Her mini appetizers are works of art. We're lucky to have her."

That was the absolute truth. With Fran's talent and drive, Eva knew she wouldn't be here much longer—especially now that Eva's family didn't even own the establishment any longer.

Unless, of course, Rafe made Fran an offer she couldn't refuse. Why that thought had her gut clenching, Eva didn't want to examine. The truth was hard to ignore, however. The distillery and everyone involved in the operating of it would move forward.

All without her.

The operation was much smaller than he'd envisioned. That bothered him. Rafe made his way up the main staircase and to the master bedroom after a stop in the tasting room, where he'd met the chef.

His new residence was going to take some getting used to. He'd never lived in an actual house before. All his previous addresses had been apartments or penthouses. Or dorm rooms.

He squelched the memories before they could fully surface.

He needed a moment to gather his thoughts. Eva's tour had given him a lot to process. For the first time since he'd made the decision to purchase the distillery and move out here, Rafe found himself questioning if perhaps this time he had indeed been too impulsive.

Sure, small was a good way to start. But he had much bigger aspirations for this next venture in his life. Only he had no clue how to go about it. One thing was certain: Eva had been right. He didn't know nearly enough at this stage about running a rum distillery. One thing had stood out to him from their tour around the property: he was going to have to be much more hands-on than he had counted on. For that, Rafe was going to need help. The foreman seemed knowledgeable enough, as did all the other staffers he'd met today. But they were each one of many cogs in a well-oiled machine. If he was going to get to where he wanted to be, Rafe needed the assistance of the machinist herself.

One Evalyn Gato.

Damn it. She'd been right. Though her delivery left a lot to be desired, her point had been a valid one. Learning this business was going to take much more than search engine queries on his tablet.

As much as he hated to admit it, he was going

to need Evalyn's help to get situated here. And it was going to take a lot more than two days of instruction from the previous owner.

She was the only solution he could think of. Despite the clear competence of the workers he'd been introduced to so far, the thought of trying to run this place without Eva around filled him with trepidation. Rafe groaned out loud and plopped himself down on the bed. What a lousy, unexpected predicament. Convincing Eva to stick around was not going to be easy. They'd gotten off on the wrong foot and she'd made no effort to hide her disdain for him.

He rubbed a palm down his face. There was absolutely no doubt that if he asked her to stick around, she would question his every decision and probably argue his every move. But what choice did he have? It wouldn't be prudent to try and recruit someone new. That would take time and effort that could be better put to use elsewhere…like an expansion of the business.

Rafe was running out of time to figure it out, one way or the other. Eva was due to stop by tomorrow morning to finalize some paperwork and round out the remaining details. Then she'd be on her way.

Rafe swore silently and sat up. The dirt and grime from walking around the property still clung to his skin. He needed a shower, and it might help to clear his head.

The master bathroom had clearly been recently renovated. A marble tub and closet-size shower stall glittered in the soft yellow light, while black-and-white floor tiles sparkled with a fresh sheen and a three-panel mirror hung above the dual sink counter.

He stripped off his clothes and jumped into the shower, turning the water to a punishing level of heat. Not too long after he'd begun showering, he heard the digital tone of an incoming call ring on his cell.

Rafe ignored it. He was no longer the harried executive who jumped out of the shower to answer a call—or worse, who had even brought his cell phone in the stall with him on occasion. Rafe had left that part of him behind. He had no interest in reviving it anytime soon. His sanity depended on it.

But he wasn't made of stone either. As soon as he stepped out of the shower, barely dried off with the thick Turkish towel, he reached for his phone and checked the received calls. He didn't recognize the number, but the caller had left a voice mail.

Rafe was surprised at the voice that greeted him when he clicked on the voice mail app. Teo Gato, Eva's brother.

"Hey, Rafe. Just thought I'd check to see how your tour went. Hit me back if you get a chance."

Rafe hit the redial button. The other man answered on the second ring. "Hey, man. Thanks for getting back to me."

"No problem. You wanted to ask about my tour this morning?"

"More or less."

What did that mean? "Okay."

"Look, this is going to sound like a strange ask, and she'd kill me if I she knew I was doing this, but I think you should ask my sister to stick around for a while longer."

Rafe sat down at the edge of the bed. What a strange coincidence. "Funny you should suggest that, Teo. I was thinking of doing exactly that."

"Yes! I knew I liked you!" Teo replied after a chuckle. "Feel like we could become good friends if you decide to stay long-term."

Rafe decided to ignore that last part. Why were Eva and her brother so intent on believing he would bail? The first part of Teo's statement rang strangely true, however. Rafe had felt a fondness for the man immediately upon meeting him, almost as if they'd been old friends who were reacquainting. "I'd like to think so."

"She's not going to make it easy for you, bro. She'll say no at first and may stick to that answer."

Rafe had absolutely no doubt about it, from what little he already knew of her. Eva Gato was stubborn and headstrong. And full of pride.

"I'm asking you to try," Teo added.

"I could definitely use her help. She clearly knows her stuff when it comes to producing rum."

"Sure does. She was responsible for the whole operation. Our old man is getting up there in years and I never played much of a part in the family business." Teo paused briefly before continuing. "I thought twice about calling you. Wasn't sure if I should. Glad I did. She may think she is, but she's not ready to walk away from this place just yet. I know it."

"Thank you for the information." Teo's input would come in handy. Rafe clicked off the call, a complicated swirl of emotions flooding his system. He couldn't help but feel touched at Teo's concern for his sister. The man had clearly been uncomfortable making the call but he'd done it for his sibling's sake. Rafe had never had someone in his life do likewise for him.

His mother came the closest, but she'd always been too busy battling her own demons. And the last time he'd seen his father had been through a toddler's eyes. He wouldn't recognize the man if he ran into him in the street.

He cursed silently again. When was the last

time he'd felt sorry for himself? These lines of thought were coming perilously close to just that. He knew all too well how futile such thoughts were and had no time for them.

Pulling a T-shirt over his head and putting on a fresh pair of khaki pants, he replayed Teo's words in his head.

She may think she's ready to walk away, but she isn't just yet. I know it.

Rafe definitely hadn't seen any of that coming. But it was always nice to have verification from the universe about his decision.

Teo had mentioned that Eva usually stopped at the tasting room before leaving work for the day to visit with her friend, the chef. Hopefully, he still had time to catch her before she left.

"You should have warned me," Fran declared, placing a tray of freshly baked popovers in front of her on the counter. They smelled heavenly. "About the way that man looks in person. Those online photos of him do not do him justice."

Eva gingerly took hold of one of the pastries, her fingertips burning. "It hardly matters what he looks like. All that matters is he now owns this place. The distillery, the house, the land. All of it."

"True. But it certainly helps that he's easy on the eyes."

Despite the steam wafting off the popover Eva could wait no longer. Her tastebuds were screaming in temptation and the topic at hand was further fraying her nerves. Utter failure certainly gave a girl an appetite. She tore off the top crust and popped it in her mouth. "Well, you'll be the only one laying eyes on him after tomorrow," she said between chews. "The less I see of the man, the better."

Fran's shoulders slumped. "Does that mean you won't be coming by often?"

She could only shake her head at the question.

"Eva, you can't mean that. I can't imagine this place without you."

She would never have imagined it either. But about twenty-two months ago, she'd made the mistake of falling for the wrong man. And now she was paying for it with everything she held dear.

Fran's gaze locked on hers. "Hasn't that man taken enough from you?" her friend asked. "Are you going to let his memory keep you from where you belong? This is your home."

Fran was wrong on that score. "It was. Past tense. The man I fell in love with took loans out on it after I gave him permission. And then he gambled all those loans away."

Victor had done it right under her nose. All the while, she'd been blinded by what she thought was love.

Eva reached for her popover again to distract herself from the depressing and guilty thoughts, but an unexpected noise behind her had her dropping it back onto the plate. Someone behind her was clearing his throat.

She didn't need to turn around to know who it would be. Why was Rafe here now? They'd said their goodbyes about twenty minutes ago and she'd watched him go up the front steps into the house he now owned. Why was he here in the tasting room?

Then it occurred to her. Of course he'd run back down here at the first chance to see if he could chat up the pretty, young chef. And here Eva was, being the third wheel.

"Sorry to interrupt," he began, his glance traveling from Eva to Fran, then back to her. He'd changed into a soft cotton T-shirt and khaki pants. The hair neatly combed off his face appeared thoroughly wet. It made zero sense, but somehow the casual, freshly scrubbed look gave him a hint of ruggedness that served to somehow up his attractiveness only further. The pulse at the base of her throat jumped as she took in the chiseled chest, which led to her imagination running away with thoughts of that aforementioned shower.

Eva gave herself a mental thwack. What was she thinking?

Rafe was no doubt thrilled to find Fran still here and he was probably trying to figure out a polite way to tell Eva to scram.

Fran was what one would describe as classically beautiful: thick blond hair, sparkling blue eyes and a head-turning figure. Eva wouldn't be surprised if Rafe was already intrigued by her. Most men were.

"I was hoping I'd catch up to you before you left."

Eva was about to hop off the stool to leave when she gave pause. Rafe's words had been directed at her, not Fran. She was certain. Her friend must have thought so, too, as she excused herself with a vague explanation about having to clean the oven before disappearing behind the swinging door back to the kitchen.

"You were?"

His lips formed an amused smile. "You sound surprised. Why is that?"

"Never mind. It's not important. What can I do for you?" *That couldn't wait until tomorrow morning*, she added silently.

He rammed a hand through his hair, as if uncertain how to proceed.

"I had a bunch of questions pop into my head in the shower. About the exact process. How you get the flavor just right every time."

All of that could have waited till the morning. But Eva let him continue. "Then I realized I was hungry."

What did that have to do with her? "You were hungry?"

He nodded once. "Famished. And there's hardly any food in the house, aside from a few staples that someone was kind enough to stock up the pantries with."

"That would have been my grandmother. Nana takes care of people. Makes sure they're fed."

"Please thank her for me."

"I will. But that can't be why you wanted to find me."

"Well, I noticed on the drive from the airport that the hacienda is near a quaint little coastal town. I thought maybe you could accompany me there. We could grab a bite to eat while I pick your brain some more."

Maybe she was being petty, but she couldn't help but goad him. "Questions you couldn't find answers to by reading up on it some more?"

Rafe rubbed his jaw, his eyes appearing to size her up. "My questions are very specific to

Gato Rums in particular. I can hardly deny that you're the expert here between the two of us."

Well, at least he was giving her that much in the way of acknowledgment.

"Go ahead and gloat," Rafe added. "May as well get it over with."

Eva bit back a sardonic laugh. How could she gloat about any of this, given the part she'd played in how it all came to be?

Still, Eva's first impulse was to say no, to turn him down then and there. But a sneaky voice crept into her brain before she could come up with some excuse. What would be the harm? The man simply wanted some company while he ate dinner his first night in town. And she was the only person besides Teo he knew on this island, as far as she was aware.

Purely platonic.

As much as she wanted to deny it, even to herself, Eva did care about the distillery and how well Rafe would take to running it. The least she could do was answer a few questions to ensure the place continued to run smoothly without any glitches in the transfer.

She nodded once. "Sure. I have no plans this evening."

The smile he returned at her answer sent awareness surging down her spine. "Great. Take all the time you need. I'll meet you outside when you're ready."

Eva watched him walk away and tried to ignore the urge to study his physique from this angle. Maybe going to dinner with him wasn't such a great idea.

Well, too late to back out now. And besides, this was barely more than a work outing. Rafe only wanted to pick her brain further about the business and the rum distilling process. It wasn't as if he was asking her out on some sort of date.

And if a small, ridiculous piece of her felt a hint of disappointment at that thought, well, that was just silly on her part, wasn't it?

They arrived in the center of town in less than fifteen minutes. Eva wasn't surprised to find it full of people and noise. This time of day, particularly on a Thursday night, always brought out crowds of people looking to shop, dine or just hang out. She noticed with no small amount of gratification that plenty of tourists were included in the number. A lot of them would be visiting the distillery at some point. That was always good for business. Then she had to check herself. It really was no longer her concern, was it?

Rafe found an empty spot on the street to park

his car. Teo had told her it was a Lamborghini, a car that screamed money and privilege—nothing like the used cars Teo bought for a bargain, then meticulously rebuilt.

"What was that sigh for?" he asked, turning off the ignition.

She hadn't realized it had been loud enough for him to hear.

"I was just thinking about how packed the tasting room will be tomorrow. There appear to be a lot of tourists in town."

If Rafe noticed that wasn't any kind of a real answer to his question, he didn't press her on it. "I guess I better figure out my way around that process as well. Greeting visitors to the distillery."

He hopped out of the car and appeared by her door to open it for her before she could so much as reach for her pocketbook by her feet. She had to say one thing about him—he certainly appeared eager to learn about his new role.

"Charming town," he remarked as he helped her out of the car.

"Us locals think so," she replied. "There are plenty of shops and restaurants, most of them housed in historic buildings built in the eighteenth century."

"I'm looking forward to exploring. I need to do a little shopping, as well."

That made sense. He probably had loved ones back in Seattle to buy souvenirs for. He might even want to stop at the jewelry shop for a lady he might have left behind there.

None of her business. Eva forced a smile on her face as they made their way down the cobblestone pathway. "What would you like to do first?"

Rafe patted his stomach. "Definitely dinner. I'm starving."

Eva had been thinking it through on the drive over, and she knew the best place to take Rafe for his first outing. There really was only one answer, as only one restaurant in town would keep her safe from the curious stares and whispered gossip. People were still talking about the poor Gato girl who'd been duped into losing her family's estate by the swindler she'd married. Being around any of that was the last thing she needed right now. It might just take her right over the edge. Worse, she didn't need Rafe to hear any hint of it either.

"I know just the place," she said, motioning for Rafe to follow.

He fell in step with her, no questions asked. Another mark in his favor. Not that she was counting.

It was a pleasant evening to be out. A gentle breeze afforded just enough of a counter to the tropical heat. The sun, slowly beginning its descent, still hung round and bright in the sky. The waves of the ocean crashed softly against the beach several yards away. To her surprise, Eva found herself happy to be out and about. If she hadn't agreed to Rafe's request, she'd be wallowing in her rented flat right about now, elbow-deep in a bowl of papaya sorbet. Or she'd be at her grandmother's cottage just off the Gato estate, letting Nana soothe her with empanadas and coconut cream pie.

The thought of all that food had her stomach grumbling. Rafe chuckled, having clearly heard. "Good thing we decided to go with the dinner first option."

Eva ducked her chin as they reached the door of the Escondido café and restaurant. The place was fully packed as usual—no surprise there—but Eva wasn't concerned. Rosa would make sure they had a table, even if it meant sitting at the server's corner. Rosa and Nana had been friends going back to their girlhood days. She was almost as protective of Eva as Nana herself was. It was one of many reasons Eva was assured none of the diners would dare risk getting caught whispering about her. Rosa would give them an earful if she heard.

The older woman caught sight of them as soon as they entered. She sauntered across the restaurant and was beside them in moments, depositing two full plates on a couple's table along the way. For someone her age, Rosa got around efficiently and swiftly, something she had in common with Eva's grandmother. Eva could only hope to be as sprightly at their age. Rosa still ran this place mostly by herself, with help from her two sons.

"Eva!" Rosa took her in a big bear hug. "Hola, *bebé*. We weren't expecting you this evening." She turned her attention to Rafe, who flashed her a brilliant smile. Wow, of course the man had a smile that could melt icebergs. "And you have company," Rosa added. Eva watched as Rosa's bright expression faded. She was putting together who Rafe might be.

"Rosa," she began through the rock that seemed to have formed at the base of her throat. This was the first time she'd acknowledge to anyone other than family that there was a new proprietor of Gato Rums.

After Eva made the introductions, Rosa led them to a table at the edge of the dining room. They were as close to being outside as possible while still having the roof above their heads.

When they were seated and Rosa had left, Eva slid over to Rafe one of the plastic-coated menus on the table. She certainly didn't need to look at one. This restaurant was one of her many "homes" on the island.

"Seems like you've known her for a long time," Rafe remarked.

"Mmm-hmm," she answered him. "She's like a grandmother to me. Just like my own nana."

Rafe pulled the menu toward him, eyeing it with curiosity. "I haven't had a chance to meet your grandmother. I hope to do so soon."

"You'll definitely be able to meet Nana soon," Eva told him. "She practically lives on the estate. Her cottage is just off the cane field." They'd made sure not to include that parcel of land in the purchase agreement.

Once again, a rush of sadness swept through her. At least that was one thing to be grateful for. For all of Eva's mistakes, at least she'd managed not to displace her own grandmother.

CHAPTER THREE

IF HE DIDN'T know any better, Rafe might think Eva was on the verge of crying. It had come about rather suddenly, sometime between handing him a menu and answering a question about her grandmother. Granted, it had been quite a while since he'd last been out with a woman, but surely he was better company than causing the onset of tears. Perhaps he had brought up a tender subject without meaning to. Was her grandmother ill? Not that it was any of his business, but he found himself genuinely intrigued by Eva.

He was trying to come up with a way to ask her about her grandmother's well-being when Rosa reappeared at the table to take their order. She inadvertently answered the question to his relief.

"Tell that nana of yours not to be late this Saturday for our Briscas game. We nearly had to start without her last time."

Eva gave a shrug of her shoulders. "You know Nana's always been on her own schedule, Rosa. But I'll try my best to convince her to be prompt."

So this nana of hers clearly wasn't ill, or this conversation between the two women wouldn't sound quite so lighthearted. But Rafe knew he hadn't imagined it: the topic of her grandmother had brought tears to Eva's eyes.

Rosa quickly took their food requests without bothering to write it down. Eva took care of ordering for the both of them, asking for two servings of black beans and yellow rice, rotisserie style pollo and two bottles of local cervezas to go with it all.

"What? No rum drinks?" Rafe asked after the older woman walked away.

Eva took a small drink of her ice water. "I figured you'll be sipping on rum all day tomorrow. You don't want to lose your taste for the stuff before you've even begun."

He saluted her with his own glass. "Smart."

She shrugged. "Just common sense."

The woman was so very quick to downplay herself. He had to wonder if there was something specific that may have caused that. Eva had accomplished a lot in her life so far. "Still, I would have ordered the rum punch. It didn't occur to me that I'd be rummed out by tomorrow."

She gave a small shrug of one shoulder. "I've been doing this for a while."

Which led him to the reason he'd asked her here. She'd just given him a perfect segue, but before he could figure out a tactful way to broach the subject, a young server appeared with two sweating bottles of beer and tall frosty glasses.

"Hey, Eva," the young woman greeted her after a polite smile in his direction. Then she proceeded in Spanish with what sounded like a question. Eva visibly stiffened in her seat and her lips tightened into a thin line. Whatever she'd just been asked, Eva clearly did not want to talk about it.

"Just fine, Elena," she finally answered in a brittle voice. "But this is a business dinner." No question, the words were meant to dismiss the other woman. If Elena was offended, she hid it well. With another polite smile, she deposited the contents of the tray on their table and turned on her heel.

"Business dinner, huh?"

She lifted an eyebrow. "That's what this is. Isn't it?"

"I guess technically."

"Technically and in every other sense, Rafe. I hope you understand that. This isn't some kind of social outing. You said you had questions about the rum. I agreed to have dinner with you so that I could answer those questions."

Looked like it was his turn to try and not be offended. "And here I thought you just enjoyed my company," he said with as much drollness as he could muster, then took a swig from his beer.

The corner of her lip lifted ever so slightly in the semblance of a smile.

"Why don't we get started with your questions? They sounded rather pressing."

He only had one ask that was rather pressing. But this wasn't the moment to bring that up. The exchange with the server earlier made it clear there were things she hadn't shared with him. Rafe hadn't come this far as a tech mogul turned investor by jumping into things blind. He had to figure out exactly what was going on before he made Eva any kind of offer.

He was going to stall. For now. "Can we eat first? I can't think too well on an empty stomach. And the smells in here are completely ruining my focus. Rosa must be one heck of a cook."

She leaned back in her chair, the smile growing wider and no longer hidden in any way. The realization sent a surge of pleasure clear to his toes.

"I'm guessing Briscas is some sort of card game?" Rafe said to further lighten the mood.

Eva nodded. "It's fun, but it takes a lot of

concentration. There are cafés around the country that have pop-up tables. You should try it sometime."

"I'll have to learn the game first." Asking her to teach it to him would probably be pushing his luck at the moment.

By the time their food arrived, Eva's shoulders had dropped about an inch. She was finally starting to relax around him.

Rafe could only hope it would last.

She did enjoy his company. That was the whole problem.

So much so that Eva had almost been able to brush away the pity she'd seen in Elena's eyes as she'd served them their beer. She'd asked how Eva was holding up given all the changes her family was dealing with. The whole town wanted to know.

Of course, she appreciated everyone's concern. But what could she possibly say to answer their questions? Had Elena honestly expected Eva to launch into a dissertation about her current emotional state? Right there in front of Rafe?

How would Eva ever be able to explain that she was racked with guilt from the moment she awoke in the morning right up until she was faced with the prospect of another sleepless night? Or the way she could barely bring herself to look her brother in the eye, let alone her father?

Yet right now, somehow, despite all of the above, she found she was actually enjoying herself for the first time since her nightmare had begun.

She watched as Rafe dove into his food with all the gusto of a man trying authentic Puerto Rican food for the first time. Her initial treatment of him embarrassed her now. Of course she'd been unfairly placing the blame for her misfortune on Rafe, when all he'd done was take advantage of a sound business deal.

But she couldn't lose sight of reality. She'd be fooling herself if she didn't acknowledge the current running between her and Rafe, or how drawn she was to him despite having just met the man. Nor could she ignore the warmth in his eyes when she caught him looking at her.

But she needed to be laser-focused right now about where she was in her life at the moment and where she wanted to go. This magnetism between her and Rafe was inconvenient and ill-timed. And how could she even trust her judgment anymore as far as men were concerned?

Betrayal sure did do a number on a girl. Especially if that betrayal came at the hands of the man she'd loved enough to marry. Victor had charmed her from the day she'd laid eyes on him. Somehow, he'd duped her into thinking that he cared for her, but all he'd really cared about was getting his hands on some money he could gamble away. But Eva had fallen for all the lies he'd fed her until it was too late and the hard truth was staring her in the face.

She couldn't even be certain now if the attraction she felt was genuine. What if it was merely being flattered that a man might be interested in her, even though she could offer him nothing? No, she couldn't risk examining such feelings. Tomorrow Eva would be leaving the only home she'd ever known, saying goodbye to her childhood memories. She'd leave both them and her old life behind. Then she had to figure out her future. The days ahead of her were a completely blank slate. It was terrifying.

Rafe cleared his throat and she snapped her head up to find him studying her. Surprisingly, his plate had been cleared.

She blinked. "Sorry, guess I drifted off."

He braced his elbows on the table. "I'll say. You hardly touched your food after the first few bites."

Eva glanced down at her own meal—food that had now grown cold. "Guess I wasn't as hungry as I thought."

"Can I ask where you were just now?"

For just an insane moment, Eva wanted to spill all of it, to confide in Rafe the way she couldn't bring herself to with anyone else, not even Nana. But she squelched the temptation. There was no use. "It's not important."

He nodded once. "You know, I listen better than most if you change your mind."

Whoa, they were approaching dangerous territory. She'd only just met him this afternoon. They'd shared one meal together, and already he was reassuring her that he could be counted on as a confidant.

It was much too fast.

Wasn't this how she'd gotten burned the last time? Victor had swept her off her feet from day one. She'd dove headfirst, following her emotions rather than her good sense.

Eva refused to risk making the same mistake twice.

"Thanks," she answered simply, crumpling the napkin on her lap and dropping it onto her plate. "You said you wanted to do some shopping? We should get to it before the shops close." Not that many would anytime soon, but she needed an out right now from this conversation. She searched the dining floor for Rosa or Elena, or whoever else could hand them their check so that they could be on their way.

Not the most subtle of avoidance tactics, but

it was the only play she had at the moment. Elena finally noticed her plight and scurried over with the check. Rafe handed her a credit card that he seemed to have pulled out of thin air. He didn't bother to look at the amount.

Moments later, they stepped back onto the sidewalk. The evening had grown colder and a slight breeze blew from the direction of the ocean, carrying with it the scent of the salty sea. A street band played bouncy Latin music on the corner.

"Plenty of souvenir shops along this street," she informed Rafe as they began to walk. "There's also Roja's Jewelry. They have a stunning collection of pearls and other baubles. How many people are you looking to buy for?"

Rafe shoved his hands into his pockets. "I'm not shopping for souvenirs. Not for anyone."

Her steps faltered at the way he'd said the last three words. His voice had been flat, resigned. "I thought you said you wanted to shop?"

"Not for souvenirs."

"Then what?"

He shrugged. "I wanted to grab some items for the house. Maybe wall art. Some things for the kitchen. I noticed there's a press for coffee. I prefer it brewed."

He stopped suddenly, then rammed his hand

through his hair. "Of course. You must have lived there yourself. And Teo."

She shook her head. "Not so much Teo for a while now. He doesn't stay in any one place for long."

"I'm sorry, Eva. I should have been more sensitive that moving into my new home meant you had to move out of yours."

Just like that, the tension crawled back into her shoulders, then stiffened along her spine.

She didn't need his sympathy or for him to feel sorry for her. "No need to apologize. It was part of the deal. You paid the asking price. All fair and square."

Great. Now Rafe pitied her as well. As if seeing it so starkly in Elena's eyes earlier wasn't enough.

He had no idea what he'd said, but Rafe had clearly stuck his foot in his mouth somewhere along the way. He seemed to be pretty good at doing that. Darned if he could figure out why. Had he picked at a painful scab when he'd mentioned owning her old house? He really did feel bad about that, regardless of the reason for the sale.

All he knew was that one minute they were chatting amicably, strolling along the sidewalk, and the next they were shooting awkward glances in each other's direction without a word between them. After they'd gone about a block farther, he couldn't stand it anymore.

Merely to fill the void, he turned to ask if she knew what might be on the tasting menu tomorrow, just as Eva turned with her own question. They both ended up speaking in unison, which just led to yet another awkward moment.

"Please, go ahead," he insisted.

"You mentioned you're not really looking to shop for souvenirs."

He simply nodded.

How pathetic that must have seemed to her. Because it was. Rafe had no one in his life to buy anything for. His mom was gone. He hadn't seen his father since the ripe old age of four. The man just hadn't come home after one of his benders, as his mom had explained during one of her own many drunken episodes. Sure, he had employees and he'd make sure Patty remained on the yearly holiday bonus and gift lists, but other than those superficial connections, there was no one.

"You said you wanted to find things to decorate the house."

"That's right."

"I was going to suggest a local artist. She has a small shop just past the town square."

He gestured in front of him. "That sounds great. Lead the way."

Within minutes they were walking through the doors of a quaint little store sandwiched between a café and a shoe shop. Rafe had no trouble picking two canvas paintings as soon as he laid eyes on them. One, a landscape, could have been a window to the scene outside the shop—the sun setting on the horizon over the ocean, framed by the beach. It would remind him every time he looked at it of his first night in his new home, his new life.

The other was just as powerful an image to his eye: a colorful phoenix rising out of the ashes, aiming for a bright blue sky.

"Interesting choices," Eva remarked as a clerk completed the purchase and took his number so that they could be in touch about the delivery date.

"You don't like them?"

She followed him out of the store. "On the contrary. I think you've shown taste with the two pieces you picked out."

He had to chuckle at her tone. "Uh, thanks, I guess. Though you sound surprised that I demonstrated I might have taste."

She shook her head, a smile dangling at the corners of her mouth. "Let's just say you've managed to surprise me more than once since you arrived on the island."

"Let me guess. You thought I'd look nerdier?"

She laughed in response.

"I get that a lot," he added.

"I must admit, you weren't what I pictured when I heard that a tech mogul had made a bid on the business."

It was curious that she hadn't seen any of the news reports or looked into him enough to get wind of all the happenings this past year. Then again, Puerto Rico was half a world removed from Seattle, Washington. It was one of the reasons he had chosen this place, after all.

And what a place it was. Rafe took in the view of the ocean in the distance, the bright oranges and reds of the sky as the sun sank lower and lower and the golden sand of the beach where it met the water. When was the last time he'd had his feet in the sand? For the life of him, he couldn't remember. So many of the past few years had been spent working, with little time for anything else.

He hadn't realized he'd stopped walking to stare at the view. Eva stood waiting patiently for him.

"Beautiful, isn't it?" she asked.

"Breathtaking. If you don't have to head back

home just yet, can I interest you in a walk along the beach?"

She bit her lower lip, clearly hesitant. "It's getting late."

He glanced at his watch. "Not that late. Come on, it'll be like walking through the painting I now own."

She eyed him speculatively. "What a charming thought."

He gave her a mock bow. "Honored to have gone from nerdy to charming in your estimation." He gestured behind him toward the water. "Does that mean you'll walk with me?"

"I suppose I have a few minutes."

Rafe tried to tell himself the pleasure and relief he felt at her answer was insignificant, nothing to overanalyze. But there was more to it than that. Rafe didn't want the evening to end just yet. He'd fully expected to be elbow deep in spreadsheets and distribution maps his first night in Puerto Rico. This was so much better than being immersed in figures and locked up behind a study door. That had everything to do with the company.

They walked across the street and down the stone steps to the beach area. Eva secured her windblown hair in a small bun at the top of her head but several wayward strands refused to be contained and fell out of the band, cascading down the delicate curve of her neck.

She kicked off her sandals and Rafe followed suit with his sneakers.

"Is the water as warm as it looks?" he asked. But Eva was way past him now, dashing toward the waves. He watched as she jumped in with both feet. Her laughter echoed over the crashing water.

"Only one way to find out," she answered.

"We don't have any towels."

"Don't need any. You're not afraid of having muddy feet, are you?"

There were worse things, he supposed. Without another thought, he joined her just as a rather large wave crashed against the shore and soaked the bottom of his pant cuffs. Make that muddy feet and slacks. Eva was wearing capris that reached just below her knees so she wasn't affected.

An older couple walked past them, waving and chuckling. What a picture the two of them must have made, splashing around the water like a couple of children. Not that he'd ever done anything like this as a child, even. There'd never been trips to the beach, no outings to have fun. Just the daily fight to survive.

That thought was perilously close to self-pity so he pushed it aside. Why couldn't he simply enjoy the moment? The way Eva clearly was. They began walking, feet still immersed in the warm sandy water.

"Can I ask you something?" she began, leveling a steady gaze on him. The brilliant colors of the sunset brought out the golden specks in her eyes. They seemed to change color depending on the lighting of the environment. It was downright beguiling.

Here it was. Time to come clean about his past. He could guess what she was about to ask him—the real reason he'd sought out a different career. A different life. How much of it did he want to reveal? The real story, not the salacious one the tabloids kept recycling.

But she surprised him with her question. "Why did you really ask me to come out tonight?"

He was about to reply when she cut him off. "And please don't try to tell me you had questions to go over. So far, none of those questions seem to have come up."

"You're right," he answered, pausing to face her. "There's really only one question I had in mind. I want to ask you to work for me."

CHAPTER FOUR

IT MADE SENSE. Total sense. In fact, she should have seen it coming. Rafe was smart enough to figure out early that he was in over his head. But there was no way she could say yes.

Could she?

Rafe stared at her, gauging her reaction. But it was hard to come up with any words. It didn't help that he looked so handsome with the sun setting behind him, the wind blowing his hair over his forehead.

"I'd like you to stay on long-term, a year or so, and then we can evaluate the next steps."

"A year, huh?"

"Six months at the least."

"I see."

"If it's a matter of another job, we can talk about which is in your best interest. Do you have something lined up?" he asked.

"There've been some prospects."

That was something of a fib. The only opportunities she'd interviewed for involved moving to a new town. Some would even relocate her to a different island. But Eva loved this town and the thought of leaving had her on the verge of tears every time it surfaced. It had been one of the major reasons she hadn't gone after any of those jobs as zealously as she might have otherwise.

"I'll match or exceed any salary," Rafe said. "But how about this as a starting point to negotiations?" He threw out a figure that had her eyes growing wide.

"That's your starting point? That high, I can't see how there'd be any room to negotiate."

He winked at her playfully and she had to remind herself to breathe. "There's always room to negotiate. And I really want you on my team."

Her steps faltered. "I'm not sure we'd work well together."

"Because you think I'm a dilettante who's only here because I was getting bored back in Seattle."

She bit her bottom lip. "Something like that."

He shrugged. "I don't take it personally. I've been called worse than inexperienced."

Eva had to wonder what that could mean. Probably that he was a demanding and harsh professional who expected the same of those around him. Those traits would no doubt rub some people the wrong way.

"Look," Rafe began. "I may be a novice to the business, but I'm a really fast learner. And I won't deny that I do need a teacher. Only makes sense that you be that teacher."

He sounded far from happy about that, simply resigned.

She didn't get a chance to respond before he pressed on. "Can you set aside your doubts about me and my abilities until I get more up to speed?"

She released a breath. "To be honest, I'm not sure that I can. I get the feeling we'll clash quite often."

"Given the way this morning went, I have no doubt. But I think we can both be professional enough to work through it."

So he was proposing a truce of sorts. But this was her life and livelihood they were talking about. Eva didn't know how she'd garner the strength to face the prospect of having to walk away from Gato Rums yet again in the future.

"What if you wake up one morning and realize you've learned all there is to know? What happens to my role then?"

He rubbed his palm down his chin, over the slight hint of dark stubble. "Fair questions. Beyond all you have to teach me, I think we'd make a strong partnership combining my novel ideas with your firsthand knowledge and experience."

She'd spent the last several weeks, day after day, coming to terms with her new reality. She'd forced herself to accept that she'd have to walk away from the hacienda and Gato Rums and figure out the next path she would chart for herself. To have the option of staying on threw in a whole other variable that vastly complicated the equation. He'd thrown her such a curve ball.

There was one more consideration as well. She was used to running the show at the distillery. Her father's word was the final one, but he rarely disagreed with her. Would she be able to handle having to answer to someone else when it came to Gato Rums?

"It could be a win-win for us both," Rafe pressed.

She rubbed her fingers over her forehead, trying to figure out what to say in response. One thing was certain—she couldn't give him an answer right now.

"I'll have to think about it."

He nodded. "Of course. You can have all night. But I need an answer tomorrow morning. After that, I'll have to look into other possible solutions." There it was, the side of Rafe that made him such a shrewd businessman. Yes, his offer and proposed salary were beyond generous, but he was also making it clear he had set boundaries.

Given all that was at stake, one night to decide hardly seemed enough time.

Her nana's house had always served as a place of comfort. Even as a child, when she'd needed to get away from her father's strict rules or the demands of all the chores in the hacienda, Eva would run there to clear her mind. And right now, she could use a bit of mind clearing.

She wasn't surprised when she walked through the door to see Teo on the couch with a cold soda, his feet propped on an ottoman.

"Hey, sis," he greeted her with a salute of his soda bottle. "Wasn't expecting to see you."

"Hey, Teo. Where's Nana?"

He tilted his head toward the small hallway that led to the kitchen. "In her usual environment. Insisted on fixing me a snack even though she fed me dinner less than an hour ago."

"I need to talk to her for some advice. It's a good thing you're here, too."

"Everything all right?"

No. Nothing had been all right since she'd said her *I do*s all those months ago.

She nudged him slightly to move over and

sat next to him on the two-seater sofa he was taking up so much of. Nana's furniture had changed over the years, but never the sense of coziness and welcome it afforded. Homemade curtains, a soft throw rug over the mahogany hardwood floor, cheery figurines scattered throughout the room… The house could be something out of a fairy-tale picture book—as could the woman who inhabited it.

Before Eva could answer her brother's question, Nana appeared from the hallway carrying a tray laden with plantains and other fresh fruit. Her eyes lit up when they landed on Eva. In an instant, the tray had been deposited on the coffee table and Eva found herself in Nana's tight embrace. It was just the way her grandmother said hello. "Eva! Hola. I'm so glad you decided to stop by."

It never got old, the way Nana always behaved as if she hadn't seen her in forever. Eva had just been here for a light afternoon siesta the other day. She squeezed into the small space left on the couch, and Teo took the hint and moved over to the upholstered chair across the throw rug.

"How was your day? Weren't you supposed to be showing that new American around?"

"That man happens to own the place now, Nana."

Her grandmother waved a hand dismissively. "Whoever he is. How did it go with him?"

"Well, that's kind of what I'm here to talk about."

Nana patted her cheek gently, her palm soft and warm. And so familiar. "You look so concerned, *mi bambina*. Tell me."

"Yeah," Teo declared. "Tell us."

A gentle knock on the door interrupted her answer.

"Come in," her grandmother called.

To Eva's surprise, Fran walked through the door. "Oh, hi," she addressed her friend. "Wouldn't expect to see you here this time of day."

"Sometimes I like to stop by to visit with Nana before heading home," Fran explained.

Was it her imagination, or did Fran's eyes linger on Teo just a little too long before turning in Nana's direction? And why did her hair look different than it had this afternoon? Like she'd taken the time to adjust it just so in a tortoise hairpin.

Fran scanned the room. "What's going on?"

"Eva was just about to tell us," Teo supplied.

Looked like the gang was all here. Just as well. The more opinions she trusted, the better. For that matter, the three people in this tiny room and Papá were the only people Eva would ever feel comfortable trusting again for as long as she lived.

She took a breath, then stood to address the room in general. "Well, the short of it is, I got an unexpected job offer this evening."

Her words were met with a round of excited gasps. *"Muy bien!"* Nana clasped her hands together.

"The offer came from the American," she explained. "Rafe Malta wants me to continue working at Gato Rums—as his operations manager. He says he has a lot to learn, and I'm the best person to teach him."

"That's fantastic, sis!" Teo exclaimed with a fist pump in the air. "I knew that man was a smart *hombre*."

Eva had to give her head a shake. "Wait. So you think this is a good idea?"

Teo's eyes narrowed on her, as if she'd grown a whole other head. "Of course I do. How do you not?"

She lifted her hands, palms up. "For one thing, it's no longer our business."

Teo lifted his head to aim his gaze at her. "That's just a technicality. You'd likely be the one making all the decisions."

She'd considered that. It might be very true—at least for the short term.

"Come on, sis," Teo continued. "You need

this—" He cut off abruptly, cleared his throat. "I mean, this place needs you. So does the American."

Both Nana and Fran were glancing from one of them to the other.

"What do you two think?" Eva asked the women.

"I think you should say yes," Nana immediately answered. "For purely selfish reasons. So I can continue to still see you every day." No surprise there.

"Why don't you ask your *papá*?"

Eva immediately shook her head to shoot that idea down. "I don't want to bother him." The truth was, she still had trouble so much as speaking to her dad without the overwhelming guilt of what she'd cost him nearly crushing her. "He has enough on his mind right now."

"Well, I'm sure he'd tell you the same thing," Teo offered.

She looked over at her friend, who seemed to have drifted off somewhere, her head tilted in Teo's direction. Was Fran even paying attention?

"Fran?" The other woman immediately snapped her head to where Eva stood. "What do you think? You haven't said anything."

Fran cleared her throat. "Like your nana, I

have my own selfish reasons for wanting you to stick around. You're my best taste tester."

So, all three thought she should take Rafe's offer. And that was before she'd even mentioned the generous salary.

"You were just saying the other day that a sign from the universe would be nice about where you should go and what you should do next," Fran added.

"Why are you even hesitating?" Teo wanted to know.

Eva rubbed her forehead and dropped back down next to Nana on the couch. "I'd be lying if I said the money he offered wasn't tempting. It would go a long way toward…" Her words trailed off. She hadn't meant to go there.

"Toward what?" Teo asked.

"Never mind. It's silly, really."

"Tell us," he insisted.

All three of them were looking at her with anticipation. "It's just—there are days I fantasize about maybe being able to purchase what we lost, that I can somehow figure out how to afford buying the place back. Maybe with the right investments, a lucky break or two…" She squeezed her eyes shut, hearing how unrealistic the words sounded when spoken out loud. "Forget it. Like I said, it's silly."

Teo stood and walked to where she sat. "I

didn't know you were thinking along those lines, sis." He ruffled the hair atop her head as if she were a small child. They were only two years apart, but Teo had always behaved as if those two years meant he somehow held rank. "If that's what you want, I'll do what I can to help. I have some money saved—"

She immediately held her hands up to stop him from going any further with that line of thought. "No. No way. I will not have you paying any more than you already have for a mistake that I made."

"That would be my decision."

Eva thought she heard Fran sigh across the room. She didn't have time to ponder what that might be about.

First things first. She took her brother's hand. "Look, it's a moot point, and not worth arguing about because it's highly unlikely to happen. For now, I just need to decide what I'm going to tell Rafe in the morning."

She was running out of time to figure it out.

Rafe pulled out a wicker chair on the back deck patio and took in the view as he sat down. He was looking at miles and miles of rolling green hills and could hear the soft sound of the ocean in the distance. The air was crisp and fresh. Not a bad way to start the morning.

Coming here, moving to Puerto Rico, had been the right decision. If he played his cards right, and things went according to plan, he could get used to feeling at home here. That would be a first for him—a place where he belonged. He hadn't found that sense of belonging with his mother, or at school or anywhere else for that matter.

But being here finally felt right.

Three days ago, he would have done anything to prevent the sequence of events that had caused that fateful night in the city. He would have given anything to keep from throwing that first punch, as much as the receiver had deserved it. But it had all led Rafe right here. So maybe it had all happened for a reason.

He took a sip from the mug of steaming hot coffee he held and grimaced as several coffee grounds landed on his tongue. Apparently, using a French press wasn't as straightforward as one might think. Too bad. He sorely needed the caffeine. Sleep had been elusive last night. Usually, when insomnia hit, he could attribute it to pressing business matters that needed his attention. Not so last night. Instead, he'd been flooded with images of a dark-haired, hazel-eyed beauty walking on a sandy beach with him. Those thoughts had led to other, more heated ones, where the two of them were doing much more on the sand than walking.

He hadn't bothered with any warm water in the shower this morning.

It was all so wrong in so many ways. If he had his way, the woman would be his employee, for heaven's sake.

"Hello?" A soft melodic voice sounded from just by the screen door that he'd left open. Eva appeared, as if he'd willed her there with his thoughts. She was dressed in a flowy yellow sundress, and the color reminded him of part of the sky last night on the beach. Her hair was done up in a neat bun and she held two paper cups with lids.

"Good morning. Is one of those for me?" he asked, resisting the urge to come right out and ask about her decision to work for him. Another reason he'd tossed and turned all night was wondering if she would turn him down, and what he might do if that was the case.

"I remembered we never got around to getting you that coffee machine." She handed him one of the cups.

"Thanks," he said, taking her offering with gratitude. "It's like you're an angel sent from heaven. Part of your duties this morning might be a tutorial on using the French press."

She pulled out the other chair at the small table

and sat down. "I already ordered a machine for you. Should be here within a day or two. State-of-the-art, makes single serve or a pot. Options for espresso, cappuccino or even cold brew."

Impressive. "Wow. Thank you."

"We can send it back if you don't like it."

"Based on what you said, I'm guessing I'm going to like it."

Rafe went to take a sip and realized the cup was completely sealed.

"You have to take the lid all the way off," Eva informed him. "In Puerto Rico, people don't actually expect you to be on the go when you have a cup," she explained. "They figure you'll sit down to have it somewhere else. Unlike the mainland, where everyone is usually on the run, we like to take time to enjoy our beverages and meals."

"Huh." He lifted the lid as told, then took a sip. A burst of sweet, savory flavor exploded on his tongue. Was that a touch of coconut he tasted?

"It's usually served black," Eva said, sipping from her own drink. "That's how I got it for you. Hope that's okay."

He let the flavors linger on his tongue before answering. "More than okay. This is great stuff. I'll have to get bags of it to brew in that machine you've gotten for me." He set his cup down. "How much do I owe you for that anyway?"

"I'll submit an expense form," she answered. "I figure it could be my first official act as your operations manager."

CHAPTER FIVE

Rafe paused in the act of lifting his coffee to his lips. "Does that mean what I think it means?"

"Yes," she replied simply, turning to look into the distance. "I've decided to accept your offer." She didn't seem terribly happy about it. Rafe decided he'd worry about that later. Right now, he was beyond relieved—elated, in fact, that she'd be joining him as he found his way around this place. Somehow, someway, within the past day, Eva Gato had become essential to him.

Go figure.

As far as the role she'd played in his restless dreams last night, he'd make sure that never happened again, now that she was officially an employee of Malta Enterprises, of which Gato Rums was now a part.

Their relationship had to stay completely professional. Both his professional and personal reputation had taken quite the hit over the past several months. He didn't need gossip about his transgressions with employees added to the mix.

Speaking of which, it would behoove him to come clean about what had happened back in Seattle, given that what she might hear second-hand, if she ever came upon it, would undoubtedly be the less truthful, more salacious version.

"Look," he began, not exactly sure where to start. He'd never bothered to explain himself before. There'd been no need. Everyone back in the States had made up their own minds depending on how well they knew him. And not too many people knew him all that well. "There are some things that happened last year that I think we should talk about. None of it will impact your duties in any way. But we should probably talk about it."

She tilted her head and waited for him to continue.

"Seattle is half a world from here." That must have sounded like such a random way to start. But Eva still seemed wholly focused, so he pressed on. "I know for most of the buyout process, I was something of a silent investor. You probably didn't even hear my name until much later in the sale process."

She nodded once in agreement. "These deals are usually handled by slews of lawyers through trusts and second or even third parties. I know this case was no different."

"That's right. So you probably didn't hear much about an incident that drew some attention about a year ago, mostly on the tech sites. It had to do with an altercation I was involved in. With someone from my past."

She nodded. "I would have been distracted with some…issues of my own around that time."

Rafe steepled his fingers on the table. Talking about all this was making him much more uncomfortable than he would have anticipated. He'd thought he'd left all the emotions of it behind when he'd moved here. "The whole thing was blown way out of proportion," he said.

She studied him. "You're right, I don't recall hearing your name back then. Not that I would have recognized it at the time."

That made sense…but not what she said right after. "But I've learned about the events you're referring to."

"You have?"

She settled deeper into her chair. "Yes. Just last night. Figured I'd do some research on the man I'd be working for."

How had he not seen that coming? "Yet you

still decided to take me up on the offer to work for me."

She shrugged one sun-kissed shoulder. "We all make mistakes," she answered simply. "You got into a fight at a nightclub. Hardly the end of the world considering no one was seriously hurt."

He swallowed, both apprehensive about the topic at hand yet relieved at her reaction. "I want you to know that was the first time I had ever so much as thrown a punch. I'm not a violent man by any means." He hadn't been, until that night when he'd been pushed too far one time too many.

Her gaze narrowed on him. "I believe you. Like I said, I don't like to judge people for their mistakes," she repeated.

Something told him that probably held true. Except when it came to herself.

She stood suddenly, then tossed her now-empty cup into the nearby receptacle and smoothed down her skirt. "Now, shall we get started?"

The rest of the morning went by in a flurry of activity. Eva went over spreadsheets, sales figures and marketing plans. There was a slew of paperwork he needed to sign.

Next stop was the bottling center. Different

labels ran through a belt with various flavorings marked on them: dark, spiced, even fruity selections like peach, mango and berry.

Rafe made a mental note to ask later about how the flavor was added. Right now, his brain was so overloaded with information he doubted he would even absorb the answer.

Plus, he was famished.

As if he'd cued her to do so, Eva glanced at her watch. "It's approaching noon. Most of the distillery shuts down at this hour. An informal siesta."

Rafe shoved his hands in his front pockets. Sorely tempted to ask her what she was doing for lunch, he resisted the urge. He was no stranger to solitary meals. A sandwich on the patio was more than adequate. "Well, I won't impose on your personal time. Go get some rest."

"Okay. See you in the tasting room in about an hour."

"It's a date," he replied, then immediately cringed. Why in the world had he phrased it that way?

Eva had only walked a few steps when she suddenly pivoted on her heel and turned back to face him.

Great. After that disastrous response, now he'd been caught staring at her retreating back.

"Do you have plans for lunch?" she asked, surprising him. Had he looked that pathetic at being left to his own devices? He had to learn to hide his reactions better.

"None whatsoever."

"Come with me."

Rafe knew he shouldn't have been so thrilled at her words. But he couldn't deny the surge of pleasure he'd felt at the invitation. "Is there another authentic restaurant you're about to introduce me to?"

She shook her head. "Even better. There's someone who would like to meet you."

That was unexpected. "I thought I'd already met all the employees over the course of the past day and a half."

She cast him a winsome smile. "Not an employee. Follow me," she ordered, turning back and walking again. "It's just a short walk. And you're bound to get a delicious meal out of it."

Curious and intrigued, Rafe caught up to her and fell in step with her stride.

Within minutes, they were approaching the door of a small redbrick cottage. The beach sat practically in its backyard, just a stone's throw away.

It might have been the most inviting little house he'd ever seen.

"I take it I'm about to meet Nana," he guessed.

"You are indeed," Eva answered. "Prepare to be charmed."

"She liked you," Eva informed Rafe as they made their way back toward the hacienda over an hour later.

Rafe's reply was a genuine, wide smile.

Nana didn't always warm up to strangers, but she'd taken an immediate liking to Rafe. So far, he'd been able to charm her brother, most definitely Fran and all the distillery employees—basically, everyone he'd met since arriving on the island.

She had to admit that he'd even charmed her. To make matters worse, Eva hadn't even seen it coming. It had probably happened last night at dinner, then some more when they'd walked along the beach together. She studied him now as they reached the stone pathway leading to the portico that held the tasting room.

A warning cry of danger sounded in her head. She remembered all too well what had happened last time she'd followed her heart and let the allure of a man lead her down a path with no return. Victor had charmed her as well…only to use her in the end, in a way that had completely upturned her life.

"Penny for your thoughts?" Rafe asked, pulling her out of the painful memories.

"Oh, just wondering what delightful morsels Fran might have come up with for this afternoon." Never mind that it wasn't what she'd been dwelling on at all, and that she'd only had that question occur to her that very second when the smell of smoked bacon traveled to her nose from the direction of the portico.

When they reached the sliding screen door of the tasting room, Fran greeted them with a warm smile. "There you two are. A tour group is due to arrive in a few minutes."

"What heavenly concoctions have you come up with today?" Eva asked, inhaling deeply the wonderful aroma.

"Kept it simple today. Scallops wrapped in turkey bacon and crisped eggplant."

Rafe chuckled. "That's simple, huh?"

Fran had six seating services set up on the bar with small plates and several shot glasses in front of each place mat.

"What can we do to help?" Rafe asked.

Fran cast him an appreciative smile. "As a matter of fact, I seem to be low on the spiced. Someone needs to run down to the cellar to grab a fresh bottle."

Eva grabbed one of the kitchen towels off the bar. "Come with me, Rafe. I'll take you down

to the cellar stockroom and show you around."
It was as good a time as any to get him familiar
with where they kept the freshly bottled spirits.

Eva led him through the kitchen, past the appliances and to the service steps that led down
to the basement. Motion sensors switched on
the ceiling lights as they made their descent.
"After labeling, the bottles head to two different locations," she explained. "The vast majority of cases are taken to the warehouse to be
shipped. A few cases come down here for use
in the tasting room."

She'd never noticed just how small this staircase was. Though they were taking the steps
with Rafe behind her, she could still feel the
warmth of his body behind her. The lemony
mint smell of his aftershave tickled her nose.

Her nerves came alive with awareness. In her
haste to place some distance between them, she
took the next step a little too carelessly. Her heel
caught and she found herself tipping forward.
Eva cried out in a panic, bracing herself for
what was sure to be a punishing fall. Suddenly,
a strong set of arms gripped her about the waist
and pulled her back before she stumbled. The
realization that she'd been caught brought tears
of relief to her eyes, until she put it together—
she was standing in a dark stairwell being held
tight in Rafe Malta's arms. Heat rushed through

her body, her skin tingling where he was touching her.

"Whoa, steady there," he said, so close behind her.

Eva took several breaths to pull herself together. Her heart pounded in her chest. She couldn't even be certain what was causing it— the way Rafe was holding her, or the fact that he'd just saved her from a painful spill. Most likely, it was both.

"Uh, thanks," she managed to stammer when she found her voice. "That was close."

"Sure was," he said behind her, his breath hot on her cheek.

"I guess I should slow down." *In every sense*, she added silently.

For several moments, they both stood as they were, neither making any kind of move or shift. Eva knew she should pull away, but something about being held by Rafe felt so right, so familiar. It made no sense, she knew. They'd just met under the most vexing of circumstances. For his part, Rafe didn't seem to be making any kind of effort to let her go, either.

Finally, she forced herself to grasp for some sanity. "I think I'm steady now. Thanks." His arms loosened around her waist, though he still hadn't fully let go of her, not until she shifted out of his grasp.

Fran was finishing setting up when they returned to the tasting room. She efficiently twisted open the new bottle and set it with the others on the counter. Slowly, their tasting guests started strolling in.

When everyone had arrived and was seated, Eva began her spiel.

"Gato Rums has been in my family for two generations," she began, then cringed. She hadn't gotten around to updating that part of the speech. She forced herself to continue.

After completing the brief intro about the distillery's history and the rum-making process, she began pouring. The tasting always started with the basic light rum and it took about half an hour to go through the different bottles.

Fran reached her side as soon as she was done.

"I'm glad you're still here for these," she exclaimed, throwing her arms around Eva's shoulders. "I wasn't looking forward to doing the first tasting by myself."

Eva returned her hug, fighting not to show the surge of emotion rushing through her. She was glad to be here, too, she realized. "You would have been absolutely fine on your own."

Fran let go of her and stepped away. "Maybe. But it wouldn't have been the same without you."

Eva smiled in response. Fran was as close to her as a sister. She didn't know how she would have gotten through the despair of the past several months without her dear friend by her side. Fran sniffled before turning away to tend to their customers.

Only time would tell if she'd made the right decision. But for right now, it certainly felt right.

How could she have even imagined leaving this place?

Rafe watched with no small amount of curiosity as the two friends embraced. That led to images of the way he'd caught Eva on the stairway. In fact, he'd thought of little else during the tasting, though he really should have been paying attention.

She hadn't pulled away when he'd caught her and he hadn't imagined the way she'd reacted— her breath quickening, her pulse jumping along her throat. Eva was attracted to him as well.

Nothing could come of it, though. He was too damaged for her.

Eva had so many people in her life who appeared to be wholly devoted to her—not a reality he'd ever experienced, not even with his own mother. Justine Malta had cared for her son, the way one might care for a... Well, a child who was simply a responsibility.

But there was never any warmth or affection. The two of them were simply in survival mode most days. Rafe couldn't really blame his mother for not having anything else left over for her dependent child.

How different Eva's life must have been in contrast. Her relationships with her grandmother, her brother and Fran clearly held mutual adoration. He wondered if she had any idea how lucky she was.

He hadn't been here long, but he couldn't imagine this place without her. The business, the haciend—any of it. She may as well have been one of the physical fixtures.

She turned to him now, motioned for him to join them. He strode over to her side. "After the tastings, we like to mingle a bit with clients so they associate a personal connection with our product. They're more likely to become repeat customers that way."

"That sounds very smart," Rafe said, though he wasn't much for small talk—especially not with strangers. "I'll follow your lead."

Fran split off in a different direction while Rafe and Eva approached an older couple stocking up on several classic, unflavored bottles. Their name tags said they were Paula and Stan.

"Thanks so much for coming to visit us today," Eva addressed them both. "You can't go wrong with the simple classic," she added, pointing to their haul.

"Really?" Paula responded. "I'm planning on throwing a Fourth of July party and want to serve rum punch."

"That will work perfectly," Eva answered her.

"She's been into those punch drinks since our vacation last year," Stan offered. "The resort had self-serve vats of it scattered all around. We've been doing a lot of traveling after retiring a couple years ago."

"Oh, how fun," Eva said with an indulgent smile.

Rafe reached out his hand to them both to shake and thank them for coming. But his mind had traveled elsewhere during the exchange. The couple had mentioned visiting a resort where the rum was apparently flowing freely. It was giving him a germ of an idea.

The couple offered their thanks and walked away.

"You might want to work on your conversational game, fella," she teased him. "You'll have to be more talkative than that at these tastings."

"Sorry, I was a little distracted."

He wasn't going to tell her why just yet. Not until he thought it through some more and weighed the pros, cons and possibilities. But he thought he might be on to something.

"Here, let's try again," he added, leading

her back toward the bar where another couple, younger this time, were still taking sips of their shot glasses. By their conversation, it sounded like they were trying to decide which flavor to go with.

"I say you get them both," he said by way of initiating a chat. Then he introduced himself, adding, "This is Eva. She's in charge of running the place."

Eva cast him a brilliant smile, evidently pleased with the way he'd presented her. Rafe had to remind himself to focus.

"I'm trying to convince him to do just that," the young woman exclaimed. "I'd like to buy both."

Rafe eyed their name tags—Kayla and Kyle. He resisted the urge to comment on that. It wasn't easy. This would take some getting used to, the social piece. Being a tech pro, he'd never had to actually interact with those who used his products. This was a whole new world.

"Two bottles seems a bit much," Kyle offered.

If he had to guess, Rafe would say they were on their honeymoon. Too bad they already seemed annoyed with each other, in a disagreement about a minor purchase.

Kayla glared at her husband. "But the bartender on the cruise we were just on said he used the spiced rum for that drink he served.

And I'd like to buy the flavored one because I really like peach."

Rafe made another mental note. Both sets of guests so far recalled drinks they'd been served while on vacation—a luxe resort and a cruise ship respectively. Interesting.

Eva stepped in then, perfectly smoothing over the tension with her suggestion. "I would go with the spiced then, if you're trying to recreate a cocktail you enjoyed in the past. Though I'd be remiss if I didn't mention that our flavored rums are award winning and they only get finer with age. You'll be enjoying them a long time."

Kyle eyed the bottles on the bar, reconsidering. "All right. I guess we'll go ahead and invest in both." His use of the word *invest* was an interesting choice, as if the man was justifying the cost to himself. Eva had known exactly what to say to convince him.

Rafe couldn't help but be impressed. Eva really was good at this. She clearly knew how to make a sale.

But if the idea that had struck him during these conversations were to come to fruition, it would take Gato Rums to a whole new level.

CHAPTER SIX

THE NEXT MORNING Eva stepped through the large mahogany doors of the main house and immediately sensed there was something different about the place. It took her a minute, but she finally placed it. One of the paintings Rafe had purchased his first night in town was hanging on the opposite wall—the phoenix rising out of the ashes. That evening seemed so long ago that it was hard to believe it was just the other night. A lot had happened since.

The art looked good there, really added to the aesthetic of the room combined with the dark wood panel walls and the colorful, handcrafted throw rug in the center of the floor. The effect was so striking, Eva had to wonder why Papá hadn't thought to hang something there himself. She glanced around the room but saw no sign of the other painting. She would have to ask Rafe where he'd hung that one.

A low, humming mechanical noise diverted

her attention. What in the world? The sound was coming from the direction of the kitchen. She headed that way to investigate. Her breath caught when she reached her destination. Rafe stood in front of a tall, complicated contraption, his back to her.

He was shirtless, his skin glistening with sweat. She debated turning right back around, composing herself and making her presence known before entering. But before she could decide, it was too late and he turned to face her. Eva had to remind herself to breathe. Heavens. The man looked like something out of a fitness magazine. Chiseled chest, sculpted arms, washboard abs.

"Hey there," he greeted her, speaking over the noise. The coffee machine she'd ordered for him appeared to be the culprit of the humming noise.

"Just back from a run on the beach," Rafe told her. "Trying to figure out how to work this thing to make a cup of strong, black iced coffee."

Stop gawking at the man and say something.

But for the life of her, she couldn't get her mouth to function.

"I don't suppose you know how it works?" Rafe asked.

Somehow her brain finally kicked in. "It sounds

like it's grinding the coffee beans. Did you read the directions?"

The smile he sent her way nearly had her focus crumbling already. She made sure to lock eyes with him to avoid staring at his sculpted, bare chest.

"Men don't read directions," he informed her. "We like to try and figure things out on our own."

"Right," she responded, with as much nonchalance as she could muster. "And how has that been working out so far?"

He answered her with a mischievous wink she chose to ignore.

With a few clicks of her phone, Eva called up the site she'd ordered from and pulled up the instructions online. Then she walked over to his side to show him the screen. Big mistake. They were a hair's width apart now, the scent of him playing havoc with her senses. A curl of heat formed at the base of her stomach and moved lower.

She had to step away, and in her haste to do so she handed him the phone with such speed that it almost fell to the tile. It didn't help that her hands were so unsteady.

Get a grip, already.

Rafe was just a man, for heaven's sake. No need to be so flustered around him. Just a handsome, successful, disarmingly sexy man. One who smelled like sun and sand and salty sea and was standing shirtless in what used to be her kitchen.

He also happened to be her boss now. As if she didn't have enough reason already to not be interested or attracted to him.

He looked down at her phone screen, then back up at her.

"Something wrong?"

The corner of his mouth lifted. "Uh, this is in Spanish."

Eva swore under her breath and took her phone back. Honestly, she was acting downright silly, like a schoolgirl talking to her high school crush by the lockers. "Right. Sorry."

Rafe chuckled. "I mean, I've been doing some studying to learn the language, but I'm afraid the owner's manual to a complicated mechanical barista is a bit beyond my abilities at the moment."

"Yes, of course," she stammered. "Here, let me."

Rafe stepped around her to give her full access. She could only hope that he planned to put on a shirt while she tinkered with the contraption. Fortunately, she had the thing running and dispensing two tall glasses of *fresca café* in no time. Not so fortunately, when she turned to hand one of them to Rafe, he was still bare chested.

Eva cleared her throat, pulled out a chair and sat down at the round center table, scrambling for something to say by way of conversation. She recalled the painting newly hanging in the foyer.

"I noticed you've hung the painting," she began.

He nodded. "They both arrived yesterday. Around the same time that thing showed up." He pointed with his thumb to the coffee maker behind him.

"It looks good there. Suits the room."

He saluted her with his cup and leaned back against the counter, his legs crossed at the ankles. "Thank you for saying so. I thought long and hard about where each should go."

"Where'd you end up hanging the other one?" Eva asked, making sure to keep her gaze focused on his face and not any lower.

"In my room upstairs," he answered, a heavy tinge in his tone. "Right across from my bed. It reminds me of the two of us walking along that very beach whenever I look at it."

The atmosphere suddenly grew thick and heated. Eva's pulse quickened as a flush crept up her cheeks. What exactly was Rafe saying? That he lay awake in his bed, remembering the two of them frolicking in the water? Heaven help her—the images she was assaulted with nearly had her rushing out of her chair to see if he might take her in his embrace the way he had yesterday on that stairwell. It had taken all the will she had then not to try and kiss him. It was taking even more now to stay still where she sat.

How much longer could they ignore what was clearly present between them? Eva knew the attraction wasn't one-sided. She could see it in the heat that swam in Rafe's eyes even now as he looked at her across the kitchen. She wasn't imagining it. Rafe wanted to kiss her, too.

The break for sanity came from a voice calling her name from the other end of the house. Fran.

Eva couldn't decide if she was relieved or frustrated at the interruption. Either way, the moment broken, she answered her friend. "In here."

Fran appeared in the doorway seconds later. Her gaze travelled from Eva's flushed face to Rafe's bare chest. Her jaw fell slightly open.

"Um, I was just wondering if you'd come taste the hors d'oeuvres I just made. It can definitely wait, though." She started backtracking before Rafe stopped her.

"It's okay. I have something I need to discuss with Eva, but it can wait. I'll just grab a shower in the meantime."

If that meant he'd come back down fully dressed, Eva was all for it.

One Week Later

"I'm still not sure how you convinced me to go along with this idea," Eva said, as they approached the car waiting for them at the hacienda gate.

Rafe greeted the driver and helped Eva into the back seat of the late-model SUV before joining her.

"What have we got to lose?" he asked her as they settled in. "Worst case scenario we spend a lovely, sunny day in beautiful San Juan, Puerto Rico. I've been meaning to visit since I got here anyway."

Barring any traffic or road delays, they should arrive in the city within an hour or so and Rafe took it as a good sign that the weather was cooperating. It would give him and Eva a chance to explore the grounds and amenities of the resort before meeting with the hotel manager for dinner later tonight.

"Tell me again," Eva said, buckling her seat belt. "This all came to you that day in the tasting room after talking to those couples. Do I have that right?"

Rafe pinched the bridge of his nose. For some reason, Eva thought if she had him repeat his reasoning enough times, he might discover some fault in his thought process. The reality was quite the opposite. A lot of his business success came from following his gut instincts, and he knew what said gut was telling him about this.

Her attitude regarding the endeavor was hardly surprising. Eva wasn't thrilled about the idea of Gato changing in any way, and as far as she was concerned, Rafe was the catalyst for any attempt at change.

Still, he'd indulge her for now. "Those couples mentioned enjoying cocktails that they still remembered months if not years afterward. Resorts like the ones they visited serve countless cocktails. They need a steady supplier of specialty spirits. We could be one of those suppliers."

Right on cue, she began her counter argument. "Establishments like resorts and hotels get their supply from the industrial-size producers. It's a mass market."

He had to agree there. "Correct. Our selling point is if we become their supplier, they can boast that their cocktail recipes use a specialty

Puerto Rican rum made exclusively in one distillery. The artisan factor."

"I have reservations that they won't see it that way."

"We just need one resort to make an offer. Others are certain to follow if that happens. I figured we'd start locally on the island, then test the waters in the rest of the Caribbean, so to speak."

"We're too small for such exclusivity," she argued.

"It will only take one large investment to start growing the distillery. Leave that part up to me. I have the means and ways to finance the growth."

Her lips thinned. "I thought you got your start as a tech mogul. You developed an app that boosted office productivity for administrative offices."

"Yes. That's right."

"And you grew the profit from that success via investments?"

Something tightened in Rafe's midsection. Despite his professional success, this wouldn't be the first time he'd been questioned about his qualifications as a businessman. Hell, he was used to not having anyone believe in him, for it rarely happened.

Yet somehow, this instance felt deeply bruising given the source of the doubt.

"Look," he began, "if I'd followed the advice of every so-called expert who told me to stick to coding—"

She cut him off. "That's not what I was implying."

"It certainly sounded that way."

She leaned back in her seat. "Then I apologize. That wasn't my intention."

He was taken aback by her words—so simple and direct, offered without any pretense or prompt. He tried to recall when anyone had apologized to him for anything and couldn't recall a single time, though plenty of people had had good cause to do so. "Thank you for that."

"You're welcome." She leaned back against her seat. "But I'm not sorry for speaking my mind. I think we're trying to bite off more than we can chew."

"Your reservations have been noted." *Several times over*, he added silently.

Eva nodded an acknowledgment and turned her head to look out the window. The ocean sparkled crystal turquoise in the distance on her side. Rafe indulged himself by studying her profile. She really was quite beautiful. Soft chin, delicate features. So far, he'd been doing a fairly good job of ignoring his inconvenient attraction to her. He didn't have any other choice. He made himself look away before risking getting caught staring at her.

Several moments passed by as they drove in silence. Surprisingly, she'd dropped the argument. Why did he get the feeling it would only be temporary?

Finally, the car pulled up the circular driveway of the beachfront La Ola hotel and casino in the heart of San Juan.

A large front patio, set up with several tables around a wraparound bar, was bustling with patrons despite the early hour. Most diners seemed to be enjoying a cocktail with their meals.

Yet another good sign.

This was a colossal undertaking.

Wasn't growth supposed to be gradual? Her grandfather had started Gato Rums with one vat and a decrepit building on a small plot of family land. They'd grown exponentially since then, but it had taken time. Rafe had only been on board a matter of days and already he was trying to take them to the next stratosphere. She had to wonder if he was being too ambitious for their own good. One thing she could say for him: the man was certainly driven. What was behind such an intense level of drive, she couldn't guess. Maybe he'd see fit to tell her one day.

For now, they were in San Juan, about to enter the first resort Rafe wanted them to pitch to. He'd somehow secured a formal dinner tonight with the resort manager.

Eva took in her surroundings as the driver hauled out their bags and handed them to the waiting bellhop. La Ola hotel and casino certainly seemed to be a popular spot, though the thought of being anywhere near a casino and its gamblers gave her an uncomfortable bristle down her spine. She had Victor to thank for that. Her ex-husband had had a strong addiction to games of chance. And he'd used her to feed his last binge—at much too high a cost.

In fact, it had cost her everything: her pride, her peace of mind, her very home.

So she couldn't explain or understand the sense of longing she felt when they walked through the outdoor lobby and she saw several couples clearly there about to begin their honeymoon. One young woman still had a costume bridal veil on, to go with her bright neon green bikini. Her husband couldn't seem to stop touching her—a brush of his hand against her cheek, his other arm draped around her shoulders. They wanted the world to know how in love they were.

Eva thought she'd had that. Victor had been affectionate and attentive. How utterly wrong and naive she'd been to believe all that had meant he'd loved her. He'd merely been using her.

Rafe's voice pulled her out of the unwelcome memories. "Eva, you coming? We're all checked in."

She gave her head a shake and followed him to the glass elevator at the side of the building. The view outside was breathtaking as they rode up several levels to their floor. A heart-shaped infinity pool was spread out below them, the turquoise blue ocean in the distance and fluffy clouds above.

She noted that the pool had a swim-up bar, which was packed with people just like the one by the entrance.

Rafe was right about one thing: they certainly seemed to be serving a lot of cocktails. Even from up here, she could see almost every adult held a beverage, whether they were in the pool or not.

The bellhop awaited them outside the door when they stepped out of the elevator. He looked barely out of his teens. Rafe thanked him and handed him what Eva figured had to be a tip. Whatever the amount was, it had the other man grasping Rafe's hand and shaking it with gusto.

She waited to be shown to her own room but the bellhop turned back toward the elevator instead. How curious. Looked like she would have to find it for herself.

"You're here, too," Rafe informed her.

Wait. What?

"I am?"

He nodded. "I meant to mention. They told me downstairs it's a suite with adjoining rooms and a shared salon. I had an admin assistant back in Seattle book it and something must have been lost in translation."

"I see."

"I did ask for it to be changed just now downstairs, but they're completely booked."

"Huh." Not ideal, but she could hardly complain. They had different rooms, after all, just a shared parlor area in between. Still, close proximity wasn't exactly conducive to her mental well-being, given how drawn she was to the man. Especially given that they'd be staying at a resort so clearly targeted to newlyweds and lovers in general.

"If it's uncomfortable for you, we can see about finding a different hotel," Rafe was saying.

That would just delay their schedule and make her look unreasonable. Besides, they'd be a whole room apart. It wasn't as if she'd have to share a bed with Rafe. She almost groaned out loud as soon as she had the thought. Why did her brain have to go there?

Eva shook her head. "No. That's okay. This should be fine."

With a nod, Rafe motioned her into the room and pulled their bags in.

Eva took in her surroundings, marveling at the luxury. Soft beige walls lent a relaxing, spa-like feel. A plush L-shaped couch laden with cushions faced a decorative fireplace.

"Why don't you look at both rooms and pick which one you'd like for yourself?" Rafe offered.

That was a no-brainer. She didn't even have to look. "I'll take the one with the ocean view," she answered, pointing to the door behind her that led to the room facing the beachfront.

"It's all yours."

Just then, the silliest and most useless thought crept into her head.

Rather than two business colleagues who were here to explore a deal, what if she and Rafe really were here as a couple? What if they were just like those newlyweds downstairs, swimming and dining by day, then enjoying each other at night—in every sense? Heat rose to her face and she felt her cheeks flush as wanton, unbidden images flooded her mind. Images of the two of them, right there in front of the fireplace on the thick throw rug. Her mouth went dry and she sucked in a rapid inhale.

"Eva?"

Rafe's voice brought her back to reality. He was looking at her expectantly. Had he asked her something?

"I asked if you wanted to freshen up before we head back downstairs," he said.

"Yes, I'd like that. Thanks."

He had no idea how badly she needed to do just that, starting with a cold splash of water on her heated skin.

CHAPTER SEVEN

RAFE STEPPED OUT onto the balcony, greeted by the sound of the waves in the distance and boisterous conversations from the crowds below. A mariachi band near the bar area played a bouncy, happy tune.

The cheerful music did little to assuage his concern. He had to be careful; he was already so tempted whenever Eva was near him and now he'd have to maneuver around sharing a suite with her.

His mind should be completely focused on trying to secure a deal here. Instead, all he could focus on was how to navigate being in such close quarters with a woman who called to him in every possible way—a woman he had no business desiring.

He felt her presence behind him, and a moment later Eva stood next to him, draping her forearms over the railing to stare at the view below.

"Wow. What a stunning picture," she said on a breathless sigh.

He couldn't agree more. But he wasn't looking where her gaze was directed. Eva had changed into a spaghetti strap scarlet red dress and the vibrant color brought out the subtle highlights in her dark hair. Her skin glowed in the sunlight.

There was that temptation again. He had to wonder if she felt it, too. There were times when he was certain of it, like that afternoon in the stairwell. Rafe knew he could have kissed her then. Everything about that moment was seared into his memory—the way her breath had hitched, the heat swimming in her eyes. She must have wanted him, too.

But other times, he couldn't be sure. She was so good at keeping her distance. Perhaps he should have kissed her that day. At least he would have found out one way or another if whatever was developing between them was in any way mutual.

"There appear to be a lot of couples here," Eva remarked after several moments.

Rafe had noticed that, too. "Nothing in the write-ups online indicated the resort was targeted or marketed toward that particular niche. Guess it must be a romantic season."

"Ah, a season for lovers," Eva said with a wistful smile. "How lucky for them."

Rafe wasn't sure what to say to that so he simply remained silent, taking in all the sounds and the scene. He knew they should stop lingering out here, should head downstairs and get a cursory look at the place—all the better to sound knowledgeable and well acquainted with the property when they met with the manager later. But he couldn't bring himself to suggest leaving just yet. He didn't want the moment to end. It felt peaceful up here, tranquil, as if they were far removed from the happenings below and life in general.

Or maybe he just wanted Eva to himself a little while longer. Eva started swaying to the music and humming low under her breath.

"You like this song, I take it?"

She smiled wide. "It's one of my favorites."

"What's it about?" he asked. "What are they singing?"

She became animated at the question and turned to face him fully. "It's about making sure not to let life pass you by. Enjoying every moment."

"Sounds like a pretty solid message."

"The major verse is all about how the best way to do that is to go on living, no matter what happens."

"To keep the past in the past, in other words."

She laughed, but there was no merriment in it. "Easier said than done, right?"

If she only knew. "I'd say so. The only reason I find myself here in Puerto Rico is to do just that—push the past back to where it belongs."

She braced her elbows on the railing and leaned forward, her gaze focused on the horizon. "Quite a life change. Must have taken a lot of thought."

"Not really. My old life held nothing positive for me anymore. Only pain." And no small amount of anger. Anger that ate him alive from the inside out. He'd had no choice but to get himself out of the toxic spiral.

"Want to talk about it?"

He chuckled at the question. "That would hardly be keeping the past in the past now, would it?"

She shrugged her shoulders. "All right. You have a point. I won't push. But my ear is there if you decided you'd like to bend it."

"I wouldn't know where to even start."

"Start with the good. Tell me how you got the idea for your app."

He tilted his head, remembering how the concept had all come about. "It wasn't one particular moment. The idea came in bits and pieces over the span of about three years."

"And you were able to bring it to fruition. No easy task."

He nodded. "You're right. Getting the idea was the easiest piece. Bringing it to life was the blood and sweat."

She *hmph*ed a small laugh. "Sounds like most goals worth pursuing."

He'd thought so. And he'd been right—at first, anyway. The app had brought him wealth and success beyond his wildest dreams…until it had all come crashing down around him.

"What about you?"

"How do you mean?"

"What good would you start with?"

"That's easy. I'd start with the time I was about sixteen or so. That's when my father really began to involve me in the happenings at the distillery. He explained the latest sales figures. Marketing plans. More detail about how the various processes worked."

"You really love what you do," he said unnecessarily. "I'm guessing you weren't happy when your father decided to sell."

"He didn't. Make the decision, I mean. It was made for him."

Her response confused him. Eva was clearly not happy about the distillery changing hands so she wouldn't have prompted the sale, and he would have known if there was any kind of silent partner. "I don't understand. Surely, it wasn't your idea."

Pain flooded her features. "No. Not my decision either. But definitely my fault. I was the reason my father had to sell his ancestral home and his family's business."

Rafe directed the same question at her that she'd asked him a minute earlier. "Want to talk about it?"

Eva blew out a sharp breath. "The short story is that I trusted the wrong man. And I wasn't the only one who paid for my mistake." Eva paused, gauging herself to see how much she wanted to reveal. She wasn't even sure why she was contemplating it. When she'd stepped out onto this balcony a few minutes ago, she wouldn't have thought she'd end up deep in conversation with Rafe about such consequential topics.

"Quid pro quo," Rafe stated. "Same goes for me. I'm here to listen if you want to get into the longer version."

To Eva's surprise, she was thinking about doing so. Maybe it was due to being up here, under a clear, bright sky. The air felt light and fresh. Breathing it in was helping to clear her mind. Or maybe it was being up here alone with

Rafe, as if they were the only two people in the world and they were standing on top of it.

Whatever the reason, Eva found herself taking him up on his offer. "I mentioned that first night at dinner that you had arrived at Gato Rums just as I found myself at a life crossroad."

He nodded once. "I remember."

"I said that because my divorce had just been finalized."

Rafe betrayed no reaction at her words. "You were married."

"That's right."

A muscle skipped along his jaw. "How long?"

"About a year. Not quite."

"I'm sorry to hear it didn't work out. How does your broken marriage relate to selling the hacienda? Did he sue you for alimony?"

She tilted her head back, a sardonic smile on her face. "If only it were that mundane. He swindled me. The marriage was a farce. For him, anyway."

Rafe turned to fully face her, then crammed his hands into his pants pockets. "What did he do, Eva?"

"He used me. What I thought was love and commitment was nothing but a ploy on his part—a way for him to get his hands on some money so that he could gamble it away." The words poured out of her. She felt part relief, part anxiousness. Would Rafe be judging her now? Would he think less of her as a business professional—or as a woman, for that matter?

"We met at one of Teo's car shows," Eva continued, her muscles quivering with tension as she spoke of her biggest regret. "My brother said Victor frequented a lot of the races and such events—a regular on the racing car scene. Teo had even seen him put money down on a classic sports car at a recent auction. My former husband gave off every impression that he was well off. Turns out, he'd never had money of his own."

Rafe let out a low whistle. "Wow. The guy sounds like quite a piece of work. How'd he pull it off?"

"By charming me enough that I was blind to what was happening."

Saying the words aloud made her sound so gullible, so lovesick that it made her naive... which of course was the sad truth.

"He convinced me to use the property and business as collateral for a major loan. He swore we needed it to invest in a major real estate venture he was pursuing, and sounded so excited about the opportunity. I loved him so much that I did it."

"What happened?"

"When the bills came due, he was nowhere

to be found. And all the money was gone. I still have no idea where he is." Pain lanced through her core. "Our divorce was handled through attorneys. Teo managed to track his whereabouts at one point just long enough for him to be served."

"Can Teo locate him again?"

The thought of so much as laying eyes on Victor had her feeling nauseous. "For what? I don't ever want to see his face again. The money is most likely all gone or close to it." She shook her head. "No, Victor can stay lost forever."

"You can hardly be blamed for feeling that way."

"I even talked my father into going along," she added with a disgusted huff. "Convinced him it was a once-in-a-lifetime investment opportunity from my loving husband. It's a wonder Papá still acknowledges me as his daughter."

"You thought he would disown you?"

"He would have had every right. My father is too decent a man." So decent he still remained on cordial terms with her mother, the woman who had left them years ago to gallivant around the globe. Eva only heard from the woman on her birthday or various holidays when she deemed it within her abilities to mail a card. That's why her closeness with her father and brother was so important to her.

Enrique Gato had not once belittled Eva for her folly, not so much as a chiding. But things between them hadn't been the same since the ordeal.

"I'd be lying if I said the whole experience hadn't caused a strain on our relationship," she found herself confiding. "There's a tension between us that wasn't ever there before."

She had her ex-husband to thank for marring her relationship with her very own family. For that, she would never forgive the man.

That's why she could absolutely not let herself fall for someone again. How could she trust her judgment when it came to love and attraction? Her one real relationship had been a colossally disastrous error. Not to mention, look at how her parent's marriage had turned out.

No, she couldn't risk being tempted by love ever again…despite the feelings she was rapidly developing for the man standing next to her on a small balcony atop the world.

Rafe shrugged on his suit jacket and straightened his tie in the mirror. He was still reeling from all Eva had told him on the balcony earlier. Her ex had certainly done a number on her.

Yet another example that confirmed a truth he'd concluded long ago: some people simply were not good. In fact, people could be downright heinous. He'd had more than his share of run-ins with such types. They had rotten souls and only served to make life miserable for those around them—even those who loved them the most.

Not that he himself had ever actually been in love. All of his relationships with the opposite sex had been brief, convenient and rather superficial. He just wasn't built for commitment.

By contrast, Eva must have been head over heels for the man she'd married. Look how much he'd been able to blind her with that affection.

Why that thought had his gut tightening, he didn't want to examine. Nor did he really want to visit the way his stomach had plummeted at her first mention of an ex-husband. She'd been so in love with this man that she'd allowed him to con her. The notion ran counter to everything he'd learned about Eva Gato. Her ex must have swept her off her feet.

Only to kick her down. A surge of anger shot through him. The man had cost Eva the security and comfort she'd enjoyed her whole life. Her family, her very home.

The more Rafe thought about it, the more his ire grew for a man he hadn't even set eyes on—anger he had to control and tamp down.

His temper would not get the best of him ever again. He'd sworn an oath to himself.

Not like the night when he'd let it take over and ruin his life with one impulsive act. Rafe took a deep breath and pushed the painful memories aside.

Eva was already out in the shared center room when he stepped out of his door. Rafe tried hard not to react when he saw her. It wasn't easy. Dressed in a silky red dress in midnight navy with strappy black sandals on her feet, her hair done up in some complicated style that accented the heart shape of her face, she looked like a stunning vision out of every man's fantasy.

He made himself look away, feigned intense focus on the gold cuff links at his sleeves. "Ready then?" He was surprised his mouth even worked.

"Yes. All set," she answered.

They left the room and approached the elevator.

"I think you should move back into the house when we get back to the distillery."

She visibly bristled, her shoulders growing rigid. "I don't need your pity, Rafe. Don't make me regret confiding in you."

Leave it to Eva to have that be her first thought at the suggestion. He couldn't really blame her for being defensive, though, not given what she'd been through. He stepped closer to her. "That isn't why I suggested it." Pity had nothing to do with it. He was simply doing what was right. The hacienda was Eva's home. He hated that he'd played any part in her having to leave it. "It's a large house. Too large for one person. Corporations provide housing for employees all the time. In this case, it's purely logical."

She eyed him with skepticism. "That's the only reason you're suggesting this?"

He nodded once. "Absolutely the only reason. I can't believe I didn't think to ask you before."

Her facial features softened ever so slightly. "I suppose it would be nice to be back in my own room."

"It's all yours," he told her. Eva didn't answer but she wasn't protesting either. Rafe would take that as a positive.

When they reached the first-floor lobby, a uniformed server awaited them and instructed that they follow him. They were led through the lobby, down a back hallway and outside to a quaint brick patio surrounded by rich vegetation. Statues of angels dotted the four corners of the square space. Rafe felt as if he might have walked into a Spanish noble's garden.

The resort manager greeted them. "Señor Malta… Señora Gato. Hola, buenas noches."

The two of them answered in turn.

"Hope you don't mind. I prefer dining out here in the evenings to enjoy the fresh air."

"I think it's lovely," Eva answered, following him to the center of the patio, where a large, round table was set for three.

They were seated at the table and a different server appeared to serve them their salads.

The next course was a mouthwatering sea bass served with lemon butter and roasted vegetables. Eventually, the discussion turned to business and the reason they were all here.

Rafe started the pitch, Eva jumping in with her expert details as needed. The manager listened intently and tried the rum Eva and Rafe had left with the beverage service earlier, first drinking it straight with one ice cube, then in a premade juice cocktail that sat in a pitcher at the table. Rafe couldn't believe the level of anticipation in his gut as he watched the other man. He'd closed his eyes after the last swallow, a look of intense concentration on his face.

To Rafe's surprise and delight, by the time the dessert plates were cleared, they'd been offered a verbal agreement to supply the next shipment.

He didn't allow himself a sigh of relief until they were back in the hallway. "That went brilliantly," he said, beyond pleased at how the meeting had ended.

"Congratulations," Eva told him with a genuine smile.

"Thanks. You, too. I feel almost elated."

She laughed. "You should. You just got your first exclusive deal."

"We both did, Eva," he countered. "I've never been in charge of a tangible product before. It's a whole different ball game."

"I have to say, you played this inning very well."

He winked at her. "I did, didn't I? Had an answer for all of his questions."

She chuckled. "Yes, indeed. Noble of you to be so humble about it."

Rafe pumped the air with his fist, perhaps childishly. But he couldn't seem to contain himself. "That couldn't have gone any better!" In his excitement, without thinking of the ramifications, Rafe leaned over to give her a quick peck on the cheek.

What happened next was wholly unexpected. Eva turned her head to speak just as Rafe's lips reached her and the result was his mouth landing square on top of hers. Rather than pull back, for a moment Rafe could only stand there in stunned silence. He waited to see if Eva would react in horror and step away. She didn't. She stood firm. Then his mind went blank. He couldn't even place who'd initiated it, but somehow he was kissing Eva and she was kissing him back.

His arms moved of their own accord and wrapped around her back. He pulled her closer, tasting her, absorbing her warmth. She tasted like berries and honey and the most tempting wine. Fire shot through his chest and he could feel her heartbeat against his. A low rumble of a groan escaped her lips and he thought his knees might buckle in response. This was madness—a wanton assault on sanity.

He didn't ever want it to stop.

CHAPTER EIGHT

Eva awoke with a start the next morning, disoriented and groggy. She'd spent the night tossing and turning, restless with an uneasiness she couldn't place. Her dreams hadn't helped—dreams of where she and Rafe may have ended up if she hadn't come to her senses and broken off their kiss. If she hadn't put a stop to their passionate encounter, would they both be here now, in this very bed?

Eva took a steadying breath, shoving the thought away before it could go any further.

Then there was the reason for this trip. Worries about the business had only added to her bout of insomnia last night. If Rafe got his way, Gato Rums would be rapidly expanding. All her life, it had been a small family operation, catering to small stores around the island and the tour groups who visited. What Rafe had in mind was a completely different goal. She didn't know the first thing about running a massive distillery. And Rafe was so new to the entire field. It would be like the blind leading the blind.

The two of them would have to work closely together if they had any hope of success. Side by side, day after day. She'd agreed to move back into the house! Eva groaned out loud. How could she trust herself to be near the man, given what had happened between them last night?

Not that she had a choice. This was her job now.

Slivers of sunlight escaped through the heavy curtains she'd drawn tightly closed the night before. The bedside digital clock read 8:00 a.m. She'd overslept. The driver would be back to pick them up at nine o'clock sharp. That gave her barely enough time to shower and dress. For the life of her, though, she couldn't seem to make herself rise off this mattress.

What was Rafe doing now? Was he still in bed? Or was he up and showered already, wondering what was taking her so long to come out of the room?

The long drive from home yesterday and all the activity must have taken more out of her than she'd thought.

Who was she kidding?

The reason she was lingering in bed was because she was delaying the inevitable. At some point she was going to have to face Rafe and the awkwardness that was sure to hover between them.

He'd kissed her! And she'd kissed him back. She rubbed the back of her hand against her lips, recalling the way he'd tasted. The scent of him still seemed to linger in the air around her. Heat shot through her as she remembered every tantalizing detail.

Ugh. She had to try and get it out of her mind. Right now, she needed to get dressed and get out there to face the man…finally.

They couldn't just ignore what had happened.

With no small amount of reluctance, Eva made herself stand and pull the curtains open. Then she went about the motions until she was showered, dressed and had her bag packed— all done in under twenty minutes.

But when she stepped out into the common area, Rafe sat on the couch wearing a cotton undershirt and loose-fitting athletic shorts. His feet were bare. He hadn't even gotten dressed yet.

Eva glanced at her wristwatch. Had she made a mistake with the time?

The smell of fresh coffee hung temptingly in the air…along with a doughy, sugary scent.

"There you are," Rafe stated, looking up

from the laptop he had on the coffee table in front of him. "I'm just catching up on some work emails." He pointed to a serving cart behind him. The source of the scrumptious aromas tickled her nose. "Have some breakfast. I took the liberty of ordering room service. Coffee, toast and eggs. And some pastries."

She stepped farther into the room. "I thought we were leaving soon. Isn't the driver due to arrive in minutes?"

Rafe shrugged, his eyes lingering on her just a moment longer than they needed to, and Eva felt her pulse quicken. He looked away, back to his screen. "I called and asked him for a delay. Figured you were still asleep when I didn't see you up and about. Didn't want to wake you."

Eva blinked. He'd thought to order breakfast after letting her sleep in because she might have been tired. She couldn't recall a single time Victor had made any kind of similar gesture. His needs had always come first.

Eva gave her head a shake. Comparing the two men could lead to very dangerous pathways, especially considering that kiss last night—the kiss Eva didn't want to bring up and hoped fervently that Rafe wouldn't either.

Thankfully, he seemed pretty preoccupied with whatever he was working on.

"Thank you," she uttered, walking over to

serve herself the much-needed jolt of caffeine.
She couldn't deny the surge of relief that ran
through her. The ride back into town would
have been straining enough, but without coffee
and breakfast first it might have been downright torturous.

"You're welcome."

She lifted one of the silver covers off a plate
to reveal a mound of scrambled eggs with fried
potatoes and roasted vegetables at the side. Her
mouth watered in response. Exactly what she
would have ordered for herself. Her gaze traveled to where Rafe sat engrossed in whatever
was on his laptop screen.

He had no idea how much he'd just lifted
her spirits by delaying the travel back to the
hacienda, nor how much she appreciated his
thoughtfulness.

For the first time in what felt like years, Eva
felt taken care of.

An hour later, Eva settled into the seat in the
back of the SUV feeling much more ready to
take on the rest of the day. She would just have
to get through a ninety minute ride with Rafe
a mere two feet away in a cramped space. Was
he still thinking about it, too? Their embrace
and mind-blowing kiss in the hallway after the
dinner meeting?

He gave no indication any of it was on his mind at all. In fact, Eva wondered if it had even registered for him, while she couldn't get it out of her head. It was happening just like it had before. The first few days after she'd met Victor she'd been enthralled, couldn't stop thinking about him. But look how that had turned out.

For her own self-preservation, she'd make sure to forget about the kiss the same way Rafe seemed to have.

Rafe interrupted her thoughts. "The hotel manager last night mentioned that we'd be driving by El Yunque National Forest on the way back."

She nodded, not sure where he was headed with this. Rafe didn't seem the sightseeing sort. "That's right. I haven't been there since I was a little girl."

"I've never been to a rain forest at all. This might be a perfect time to rectify that. Any interest in stopping?"

Guess she'd pegged him wrong about the sightseeing part. "We have quite a lot of work ahead of us," she responded, adding silently, *thanks to your aspirations for Gato Rums.*

"All the more reason. Who knows when I'll get a chance to visit again?" At her hesitation, he prodded. "Come on, I'm sure the foreman and rest of the crew have a handle on the distillery.

He can manage being in charge for another few hours. With Fran's help."

True enough, but something about experiencing yet another adventure with Rafe had her feeling unsettled. Strolling through the lush rain forest, surrounded by all that vegetation and wildlife… Those were the types of activities that led to lasting memories. She didn't need too many of those that featured the man sitting next to her.

She turned to find Rafe staring at her expectedly, still awaiting her answer. As leery as she was, Eva was going to agree to go. After all, if there was even the possibility that Victor was the reason she was hesitating to do something, she couldn't let that stand. The man had taken enough from her. Besides, it was hardly a romantic and intimate outing. They'd be visiting a national park, for heaven's sake.

She shrugged one shoulder. "Sure. Why not. Let's go."

Rafe grabbed her hand and gave it a gentle squeeze, appearing thrilled at her answer. That sent a shiver of pleasure down her spine. He leaned over to communicate the change in plans to their driver.

Less than half an hour later, they turned into the road that led to the national park. She hadn't exactly planned for a day hiking through slippery trails. Thank the saints she'd worn comfortable flats.

The driver dropped them off at the entrance with the understanding that he'd be back to get them in a couple of hours.

A chorus of sounds rang in the air as they walked through the park: several different bird songs, the hum of running water over the falls and simply Mother Nature in general.

Flats or not, the pathway was wet and slippery; Eva stepped gingerly and walked slowly. To his credit, Rafe didn't seem to mind her speed, as he was taking in his surroundings and appeared totally engrossed. For that matter, so was she. Why hadn't she made her way back here over the years? The forest was magical, as if they'd stepped onto an entirely different planet.

He cupped a hand to his ear. "Is that—"

She chuckled, cutting him off. "Yes, what you're hearing is the native coqui frog. This is their natural habitat."

He returned her laugh with one of his own. "Go figure. It really sounds like that's what they're saying."

"If we're lucky, we might even catch a sighting of one, though they're very shy creatures."

"I'll keep my fingers crossed."

"If we're really lucky, we might lay eyes on a parrot."

He chuckled. "Why would seeing a talking bird make us lucky?"

"Because this would be the rare Puerto Rican Parrot. The only place they call home is here on the island."

"Huh. All right then, I'll keep my eyes open for bright green birds who might be chatty."

She laughed at his description. "Bad news is, they're endangered. Only a few hundred left."

Rafe rubbed his chin. "That's too bad. Then the odds of seeing one are probably low."

Eva resumed walking down the path. "There have been sightings. Legend says seeing one will lead to good luck and fortune. That's what Nana told me, anyway."

As if on cue, a flock of colorful birds flew overhead, gliding majestically through the sky. None of them were the coveted parrots, however.

Rafe pointed up. "I don't suppose…?"

"Afraid not. Keep looking. Like Nana always says—keep your eyes open and your heart full of hope."

She'd have done well to heed that first part before getting married. The thought of Victor dulled her mood, so she pushed it—and him—

aside. It was too beautiful out here to dwell on regrets.

When they got to a waterfall, they watched the more adventurous types who were rock jumping into the lake below.

"I might have to try that someday," Rafe said next to her. An unbidden image flashed into her mind before she could stop it—Rafe holding her hand as they leaped off the edge of a cliff into the warm pool of water below. The two of them holding on to each other while swimming... Eva blinked the picture away before it could go any further. What was wrong with her? So much for seeing the rain forest as less than romantic. Then again, Rafe seemed to elicit such thoughts from her no matter where they were.

Before long they'd reached the opening that led to the Torre Britton, an observation tower that afforded panoramic views of the park and the neighboring mountains. The structure was surrounded by visitors. Tourists flocked to this location as one of the top attractions on the island, though Eva figured just as many of them could be locals, given the amount of Spanish she could hear.

She turned to Rafe. "Do you want to go up?" It was a pointless question. Eva knew with one-hundred-percent certainty what his answer would be.

"You have to ask?" he said, his smile widening. He tugged on her hand, then sprinted to the tower, keeping her hand in his as they climbed the stairway. In his haste, he probably just wanted to make sure she kept pace with him—nothing to read into. Still, it was a challenge to ignore the electric current that sparked where their skin touched.

When they reached the top, Rafe was barely out of breath, while Eva had to pause to catch hers…only to have her breath taken away again when she caught sight of the view. It was beyond magnificent: miles and miles of lush greenery, colorful birds dotting the bright blue sky, the majestic mountain in the distance. The air was clear and crisp, so fresh she could almost taste it with every breath.

"Wow," she heard herself utter.

"I can't think of anything better to say," Rafe answered quietly next to her.

"I guess I didn't appreciate all those years ago what a rare sight I was looking at. This is amazing." She might have never thought to visit this part of Puerto Rico if it hadn't been for Rafe.

"Aren't you glad I suggested coming?" he asked, as if reading her thoughts.

She was, truly. "I am. Thank you. I'll admit

that you were right. About this, anyway," she couldn't help but add.

Rafe's eyes held merriment and curiosity when he turned away from the view to look back to her. "All right, I'll bite. What is it that you think I'm incorrect about? Though I'm fairly certain I know the answer."

"I think the expansion might be more difficult that you think."

He dropped his head. "Ah, I was right. That would have been my first guess."

"We're just not there yet, Rafe. Gato isn't big enough to become such a major supplier. I don't know that we ever will be."

Rafe returned his gaze to the view of the horizon before answering her. "If I didn't know any better, I might think you're doubting your abilities to adapt to a more demanding role."

Eva was taken aback by his suggestion. "My trepidation does not come from lack of confidence, Rafe."

"Are you certain?"

"Yes," she answered, perhaps a little too quickly, though a hint of doubt had slithered into her mind. Darn Rafe for putting it there.

"I think your self-confidence took a big hit because you made one bad decision. Granted, it resulted in dire consequences, but you're letting that cast a shadow over your entire future."

Was that what she was doing? Living in a shadow? She immediately tossed the notion aside. No, Rafe couldn't be right. Her betrayal at Victor's hands had nothing to do with her apprehension about this expansion. That was just common sense on her part. She was certain they'd be biting off more than they could chew.

Rafe just didn't know any better.

Rafe feigned interest in his cell phone screen as they drove in silence back to the hacienda.

He never should have kissed her. And he certainly shouldn't have tried to scrutinize her mentality the way he had up at the viewing tower.

Eva was still hurt and bruised from the calamity that had been her marriage. It was one thing to nudge the woman out of her comfort zone when it came to business. But Rafe had absolutely no right to share his opinions about her personal life.

Given that he was much too damaged to risk any kind of relationship himself, he had no business toying with her emotions by losing control enough to kiss her. So why couldn't he stop thinking about the way she'd tasted? The way she'd felt in his arms? Rafe let out an ironic laugh and turned to stare out the window.

He was so good at doling out advice. If only he could take some of it to heart himself.

His new home and environment were definitely helping. He'd be a fool to risk having it go south in any way because he couldn't resist the temptation that was Eva Gato.

The day had grown cloudy by the time they turned in to the gravel driveway of the Gato hacienda. Eva hadn't done much talking during the ride, and for the life of him he couldn't think of much to say either. If only he'd kept his mouth closed when it had mattered, back at the tower. But he'd wanted so badly to tell her what was so obvious to him: that she was a talented, smart, accomplished woman. A beautiful one, at that. The only reason Eva doubted herself or her abilities in any way was because of what that scoundrel had done to her.

What was wrong with him? Regardless of his attraction to her, Eva was his employee. He had zero right to speculate about anything beyond her duties as his operations manager. If she had doubts about his business plan, they could sit down and discuss her reservations and come up with ways to address each one.

So that's what they would do. First thing tomorrow morning, he and Eva would sit down and develop a project plan based on all the concerns she had regarding Gato Rums becoming a supplier to an exclusive San Juan resort, with many more resorts to follow if Rafe got his wish.

He needed Eva's help if he wanted to be successful with this venture and Rafe knew without a shred of doubt that Eva would meet any challenge the expansion might bring.

Eva just had to believe it, too.

CHAPTER NINE

Nassau, the Bahamas, Two Weeks Later

DESPITE BEING A native daughter of Puerto Rico, Eva still shivered when stepping out of the hot sun and into a highly air-conditioned building. The sudden drop in temperature never ceased to shock her momentarily, though one would think she'd be used to it having lived on a tropical island for most of her life. It was no different now as she stepped into the lobby of the New Paradise Hotel and Resort, the next establishment on their list to try and recruit as a buyer. Rafe had been right: once the manager in Puerto Rico had signed on, other establishments had indicated interest in hearing their pitch.

The lobby was decorated to look like an underwater city and the entire wall behind the reception desk was a functioning aquarium full of colorful fish.

Eva took it all in as Rafe went to check them in.

"I'm afraid it's another suite," he told her when he returned to her side.

Pretty standard setup at these resorts, apparently. She would be sure to handle it better this time, though. For one, Eva would make sure to spend as little time in the suite as possible. Less chance of running into Rafe as he exited the shower or returned sweaty and breathless from a morning run. And less chance of another unplanned kiss.

They were only here for three days. How hard could it be? The resort manager had insisted they stay on after their meeting as his personal guests, regardless of which way the negotiations went. Eva suspected the man's generous invitation had less to do with rum purchases and more with finding out who Rafe was and learning about the app he'd created.

Since their trip to San Juan, she and Rafe had developed something of a solid working relationship. Though she wasn't entirely convinced about his plan to take Gato Rums to a higher stratosphere, he'd made her feel less anxious by taking the time to chart out his exact goals for the expansion and the way he intended to finance those goals. One thing was certain: if the distillery was to exclusively supply several resorts with their rum, there would be some major investments that needed to be made, everything from purchasing more equipment to hiring new staff.

He'd certainly made it sound doable. So she would reserve judgment. For now.

A bellhop relieved them of their bags and they made their way down a concrete path to their accommodations. The golden sand of the beach glittered in the distance and a gentle wind alleviated a small amount of the heat. A sideways-walking land crab moved by her toe into the nearby bushes. This place had an apt name, as it really was something of a paradise.

Much like the hotel in San Juan, there appeared to be a lot of newlyweds. Just a cursory glance around showed her several couples holding hands, feeding each other at the outdoor tables or frolicking in the pool together.

"I guess resorts are popular places for honeymooners," Rafe commented, clearly thinking along the same lines.

"Not surprising," Eva answered, hating how wistful her voice sounded. Her own honeymoon had left her tired and frazzled by the time it was over. "Considering what a romantic and relaxing time these resorts offer."

"Is this the kind of place you flew off to after getting married?" he asked. His eyes were hidden behind shiny aviator sunglasses with a gold rim.

Eva laughed with a bitter tone. "No. Victor insisted we go to Las Vegas. That should have been my big clue about how he liked to spend his time." She'd been blind to so much—foolishly so.

The layout of the suite was quite similar to the one they'd shared in San Juan. A wet bar stood in the back corner of the room, while a flat-screen TV hung above the mantel. A sliding glass door led to a balcony overlooking the beachfront. The bedrooms were set up to look like the cabin of a boat, complete with fake portholes in the wall.

After freshening up, Eva left her room to find Rafe had already changed. He stood staring at a promotional video about all the attractions the resort had to offer.

"So I was thinking," he began when he saw her. "We don't meet with the bar manager until morning. I say we take the time to check out the property and take advantage of some time in the sunshine while we're here."

Eva couldn't think of a possible reason to say no to that, so moments later, they were standing at a tall table in the bar being served the resort's signature cocktail. The menu said it was called New Paradise tropical iced tea. It tasted divine, a burst of fruity flavor on her tongue.

Rafe seemed to be enjoying it also, as his tall glass was already halfway empty. She studied him, trying not to be discovered doing so. The lines of tension along his lips seemed to have softened; his breath was steady and slow, and he appeared much more at east than he had those first few days after he'd arrived. In fact, she'd noticed him becoming more and more relaxed with every passing day back in Puerto Rico.

"What made you do it?" she asked, surprising herself. She wasn't aware that she'd even intended to ask the question. Maybe it was the tropical iced tea. "What made you leave your life behind to move to an island and into an entirely different career? Did it have anything to do with the incident you referred to that first morning after you arrived?"

Rafe leaned his elbows on the small table. The action brought them practically nose to nose. She could smell the citrus scent of his aftershave, the mint on his breath.

"Let's just say it was the proverbial straw that broke the camel's back."

"Must have been a very heavy straw." Why was she pushing this line of conversation? Rafe hadn't been very forthcoming about what had happened back in Seattle that had him replacing his whole life with a new one. The articles reported that he'd been involved in a late-night brawl, Eva didn't know how much might be mere gossip.

"I guess you could say that," he responded.

"There must be people back in Seattle who miss you," she prompted.

His eyes clouded over as he shook his head. "Nope. Afraid not. Not a single person."

He'd implied as much that first night when they'd gone shopping in town. Eva set her glass down. "How can that be?"

"It was just me and my mom growing up. She's gone now. And coding is a very solitary career. I didn't make a lot of acquaintances."

"What about girlfriends?" She cringed as soon as the words left her mouth. Such a personal question, but she was genuinely curious. How could someone like Rafe Malta not be attached to a woman at all times? He was successful, devilishly handsome and wealthy.

"I was seeing someone rather casually for a few months. She didn't like the unwanted attention of a scandal while she was auditioning to replace the lead in an Australian soap."

An actress, then. She must have been exceptionally beautiful. Not surprising, considering what a catch Rafe would be considered by most women. A twinge-like sensation ruffled in her middle, but she refused to acknowledge it as any kind of jealousy.

Rafe held his glass up in a mock salute to her before taking a large swig. "So, no one. That would be the correct answer to your question about who might be missing me."

Maybe she was pushing, but Eva couldn't seem to stop herself. "Would you have invited her to come with you to Puerto Rico otherwise?" The thought of Rafe showing up that day with a woman by his side made her shoulders tighten, and Eva shivered at that thought. How out of place she would have felt as a third wheel, how awkward and uncomfortable.

Why was she punishing herself by pursuing these questions?

Rafe's reaction was immediate. "Absolutely not. No. The relationship wasn't that serious, for one." He answered her question with a clear shudder. "Our split was just another step on the way to making my decision. There was nothing and no one left for me to stay in Seattle for."

The words *I'm sorry* hovered on the tip of her tongue, but they seemed oddly inappropriate for the moment. Before she could think of anything else to say instead, Rafe ordered another round for them.

Eva made a mental note to go slowly with her second. The bartender had been rather generous with the spirits and she needed her wits about her being alone with Rafe—especially considering they'd be returning to the same suite yet again at the end of the evening.

They didn't need a replay of what had happened in San Juan.

Rafe couldn't recall the last time he'd felt this relaxed, this carefree. A man could get used to this vacationing-on-a-tropical-resort thing. Though something told him his present company might have something to do with how much he was enjoying himself.

He studied Eva now over the rim of his glass. Dressed in a spaghetti strap cropped tank that showed just enough of her tan midriff and a colorful sarong, she was turning more than a few heads in their direction. Rafe couldn't seem to take his eyes off her himself, for that matter. The woman was downright striking. Did she even know it? He suspected not.

Steady there, fella. She's your most important employee.

How many times did he have to remind himself to avoid such thoughts about her? But that was becoming more and more difficult to do with each passing day in her company. Especially when he remembered the way her lips had tasted against his, and the way she'd felt in his arms. Three days didn't seem like a long time on a calendar, but it could be an eternity when one was faced with constant temptation.

More than once, he'd caught himself wondering how things might have been different between them if they'd met under any other circumstances. Rafe suspected he would have fought harder for Eva if she'd been the woman he was dating back in Seattle.

The train of thought led to other questions that unnerved him. How might Eva have reacted if she'd been the woman with him that night? If she'd seen the way he'd behaved after losing his temper?

The relaxation he'd been enjoying only moments ago flushed away like a dam had been demolished. Unwanted images snapped through his mind before he could stop them: The flashing lights of patrol cars. Cuffs snapping onto his wrists. Black ink on his fingertips. Pain and regret surged through his core. Eva's voice interrupted his thoughts in the nick of time, before he could spiral further down the hole of dark memories.

"And where did you just drift off to?" she asked, concern and curiosity clouding her eyes.

"Trust me, you do not want to know."

She lifted one eyebrow. "You sure? Because

wherever it was, it had you cursing quite bitterly."

He hadn't realized he'd said the explicit words out loud. "Sorry."

Her lips curved into a small smile. "What are you apologizing for? Zoning out just now? Or for cursing?"

Rafe couldn't even be sure. "Take your pick. I'll let you decide."

Eva's smile turned to a chuckle. "Well, if it's the latter, I'll have to remind you that I grew up with an older brother who's fairly active in the very male dominant world of sports car racing. Plus, I also grew up around field and factory workers who often let go of any polite pretenses at the end of a long and laborious day. My ears are accustomed to naughty words. Not to mention, I did my own fair share of cursing when I realized what a charlatan I'd married."

He tapped two fingers to his forehead in a salute. "Got it. No apologies necessary for colorful language."

What a pair they made—Rafe still licking his wounds from the ramifications of his own actions, and Eva still recovering from her sham of a marriage. Maybe that was why he felt such a strong connection to this woman he'd only met a few short weeks ago. None of it should have made any sense. All he knew was that he felt right talking to her, sharing things about his past he wouldn't dream of speaking of to anyone else. And he didn't want to leave her side just yet.

They'd both gone silent, but no awkwardness hung in the air between them. It was as if no more words needed to be spoken in the moment. The afternoon had grown darker, evening settling in around them. He was about to polish off his drink when a loud cheer erupted behind them, followed by the loud roar of applause.

Eva's head perked up in the direction of the noise. "Sounds like some kind of show."

A chorus of oohs and aahs echoed in the air.

"An impressive one from the sound of it," he replied. "Let's go check it out." He could use some kind of distraction.

Eva followed Rafe down a sandy, wooden pathway toward the beach. The raucous noise grew louder as they approached a pavilion stage near the water and a drumroll began to play just as they reached the crowd.

She gasped when she saw what all the commotion was about. The performer on stage held a torch alight with fire. Astonished, she watched as he put the entire flame in his mouth.

When he was done, he turned to the audience. "Want to see that again?" he asked, smiling and seemingly unscathed. "How about bigger this time?"

She joined the others in enthusiastic applause as the fires he lit grew larger and larger. Effortlessly, he swallowed each one.

"How does he do that?" she asked Rafe, incredulous at what she was watching. How exactly did one train to become a fire-eater?

"The man must have a steel pipe where his throat ought to be."

By the fourth flame, Eva didn't think she could handle watching much more. The fire was the size of a traffic cone at that point and she could have sworn she felt the heat of it even at their distance from the stage. Mercifully, the man finally took a bow and waved to the audience. Everyone responded with a much-deserved standing ovation.

"Oh, thank heavens," Eva muttered, hand to her chest.

A tuxedoed MC appeared on stage with a microphone to announce a reggae band would follow as the next performance.

"A fire-eater is going to be a tough act to follow," Rafe announced as they watched the four musicians set up.

Within moments, they were listening to the upbeat sounds of island pop music. Several people hopped onto the makeshift dance floor in front of the stage.

To her surprise and, admittedly, to her delight, Rafe straightened and offered her his hand. "How about it?" he asked, his smile sending a shiver along her skin. "Dance with me?"

Despite having nursed it, Eva figured the drink back at the bar had to have gone straight to her head. Why else would she be taking Rafe up on his suggestion? She took the hand he offered and followed him down near the other dancing couples.

Dancing with Rafe was so not a good idea, and hardly a professional activity covered in her job description, but it was hard to contain her enthusiasm.

In her defense, it had been so long since she'd danced with a man. Victor had declined most opportunities to do so during their brief time together, protesting that he had no rhythm and possessed two left feet. Now that he was gone and out of her life, Eva could see his many refusals for what they were: signs of a narcissist who refused to step out of his comfort zone for anyone else's benefit.

Eva began swaying to the bouncy tune. To her surprise, Rafe was impressively coordinated and completely in step with the beat. A man of many talents. She wouldn't have pegged him as the dancing type.

"You've been holding out on me," she yelled over the music. "You never mentioned what a good dancer you are."

He winked at her and it sent a wave of pleasure through her center. "In my late teens I worked as a busboy at a grunge club in Seattle," he told her, his voice raised above the noise. "Sometimes the bands booked at the venue stayed on and kept playing after closing. The rest of the staff and I took advantage of the free private shows."

"Grunge, huh? Not a lot of that playing in Puerto Rico or the Bahamas."

"The music may be different, but some dance moves are universal," he told her. To demonstrate, he took her by the wrist, then twirled her. Laughter bubbled up from Eva's throat as he proceeded to spin her around in a slow circle, then dipped her low. The gentle breeze felt like a caress on her cheeks and the salty scent of the ocean tickled her nostrils.

Eva soaked it all in: the joyful noises around them, the pulsing tempo of the music, the pure glee of dancing on the beach.

Heaven help her, she was having fun! For the first time in about two years, she was actually allowing herself to just enjoy the moment. Reality would come soon enough.

A low voice in her mind nagged that she had no right. How could she be out here enjoying herself as if she hadn't a care in the world?

After what she'd done to her family.

Her step faltered and she felt herself tipping. Rafe reached out and grabbed for her before she could stumble. Suddenly, Eva was sprawled against him, held tight in his arms, her cheek resting on his shoulder just as the song ended.

The band wasn't silent for long. Before Eva could make any kind of move to step away, it started up a reggae version of a traditional tango song.

Rafe straightened. His arm went around her upper back, and he held her other hand in the air in the classic beginning position.

"You'll have to help me out with this one," he said, his eyes darkening on her. "I can't say I've ever done the tango before. I'm guessing you might have, though."

Without thinking, Eva led him through the first few steps. He got the hang of it in no time. Then they were dancing like two familiar lovers, matching each other move for move.

The thought brought a rush of heat to her cheeks and her heart hammered against her chest. They could have been the only two people on the beach in that moment. Moving with him this way, so intimately, felt right and real… even as alarm bells rung in her head that she had to stop whatever was happening between them.

But right now, she felt powerless to do so.

Finally, the song ended and they were surrounded by silence for several beats. Then a chorus of voices erupted around them and Eva became remotely aware that they'd somehow garnered attention from their fellow dancers who were applauding and cheering them. The noise hardly registered in her ears, though, the pounding in her head drowning out all else. Her vision had narrowed to a tunnel. Only Rafe remained in her focus. Heaven help her, if he tried to kiss her now, she would let him. Despite the slew of people around them, she would lean into his kiss and return it.

Stop it.

On shaky legs, she finally forced herself to pull away. Rafe cleared his throat, then crammed his hands into his pockets. "That was, uh…" He trailed off, then looked off to the side and the gentle crashing waves.

She'd be hard-pressed to find the appropriate words herself. There was no point in even trying.

"I think I've had enough dancing for tonight,"

she stammered out. There was no way they could continue. The next song playing was a soft ballad that had everyone around them slow dancing in each other's embrace. "I'm suddenly very tired." They both knew it was a lame excuse, but it was all her scrambled mind could come up with.

Something shifted behind Rafe's eyes. He motioned for her to lead them off the makeshift dance floor.

When they reached their suite, she didn't bother to linger in the common area.

"I think I'll order room service," she said, making her way hastily to her door. "If it's all the same to you. All that spontaneous dancing has left me rather beat."

"Of course," he replied, his voice gravel rough. "Whatever you prefer."

She nodded, certain that he wasn't buying the excuse but grateful he wasn't asking any questions about her sudden bout of fatigue. "Then I'll see you in the morning. Good night, Rafe."

She stepped into her room and shut the door before he could so much as return the pleasantry. It took several moments to regain her shaky breath.

Rafe was up earlier than he would have liked the next morning. He had no idea what he might say to Eva when he saw her. Lines had been blurred yesterday in a way that had confused and rattled him. Their kiss in San Juan had been easy to dismiss. It had been a spontaneous moment, coming about by accident.

Dancing together yesterday couldn't be so easily downplayed. He'd lain awake half the night trying to process exactly how to address the proverbial elephant in the room. There was an electricity of attraction between him and Eva that was becoming more and more difficult to ignore.

If he was confused, Eva had acted downright skittish.

They still had to get through this meeting with the resort's food and beverage director.

Rafe poured his second cup of coffee and had just started rehearsing his pitch mentally when Eva stepped out of her room, greeting him with a hesitant smile.

Damn it. This was exactly what they didn't need—this tension and sense of awkwardness between them. He thought of all the reasons he should have kept his hands off of her last night. As soon as the music had changed to that tango tune, a dance that required intimate contact, he should have simply declared the dancing over and stepped away.

"Good morning," he offered.

"Morning." She pointed to the serving tray. "Thanks for ordering coffee already."

"Sure thing."

Dressed in an emerald green button-down shirtdress, cinched at the waist, and strappy leather sandals, she looked freshly scrubbed and ready to tackle the day ahead. He had to hand it to her. The outfit she wore was the perfect balance, professional enough for a business meeting yet casual enough so that she didn't stick out at an island resort.

Then again, the woman would look good wearing a canvas sack. Or wearing nothing.

He swore silently. *Don't go there.*

Fifteen minutes later, they were seated at an outdoor picnic table by a crystal blue infinity pool. Paolo Bertrand had been the New Paradise beverage and food director for over ten years. A heavyset man with thinning hair and a thick mustache, he had a warm smile that immediately made them feel welcome. Like in San Juan, Rafe started with the numbers part of their spiel. Then Eva took over with her detailed knowledge of the rum and all the distinctive taste patterns Gato Rums could provide for the resort's cocktails.

The meeting went well enough, but unlike the last one, they weren't able to secure any kind of agreement, though Paolo assured them he would get back to them within a week or so. Rafe had been in business long enough to know that not every decision maker would have an answer immediately, but he would have much preferred to walk away with an understanding and signed paperwork.

"What do you two have planned for the rest of the day?" Paolo asked, escorting them back to the resort lobby.

"Hadn't really thought about it past this meeting," Rafe answered.

The other man clasped a hand to his chest with no small amount of exaggeration. "Oh, but you cannot waste this beautiful day in paradise." He turned to Eva and shot an imploring look to her as well.

"What do you suggest?" Eva asked him.

"There's so much to do," Paolo declared. "Snorkeling, parasailing. Or the excursion we're known for here—Calypso Island."

Rafe recalled reading briefly about the small island a few miles off the beach. It had been established as both a tourist attraction and a habitat for several flora and fauna species. The resort offered daily boat rides there for small groups of tourists. Beyond that, Rafe didn't know much else about it.

"What's Calypso Island?" Eva asked.

"An exotic wonderland," Paolo answered, "home to several species of wildlife and fauna indigenous to the Bahamian islands. Exotic birds, rare wildflowers and the endangered cyclura lizard. You can't come here and not visit."

Eva returned the man's wide smile, clearly charmed by his enthusiasm. "I'm definitely intrigued," she told him, glancing at Rafe with question.

They had a whole day ahead of them. At the very least, such an outing would distract them from the awkwardness that was sure to appear once the two of them were alone again.

"I'm game if you are," he answered.

Paolo clapped his hands together. "Fantastic. My nephew is captaining the boat this afternoon. I'll call him to let the crew know to expect two last-minute guests."

The three of them shook hands and Paolo bid them goodbye, leaving them by the check-in desk.

"That's the afternoon sorted, then," Eva offered as they stepped out into the brilliant sunshine. The day had grown considerably hotter, with little to no breeze. The ocean in the distance was waveless, dotted with swimmers trying to cool off.

"Not a bad way to spend an afternoon like this one," Rafe said, rolling up his sleeves and unbuttoning the top two buttons of his shirt. So far, the island temperatures since they'd arrived had been fairly comparable to the Puerto Rican clime.

"And I've never seen a Bahamian cyclura lizard before."

"Neither have I," he offered rather lamely.

Good thing they had found something to do, Rafe thought. Their small-talk game was swiftly becoming pretty dry.

Now they just had to get through the rest of the morning.

CHAPTER TEN

THE BOAT RIDE from the resort to the mini refuge island took less than ten minutes.

"Enjoy your explorations," a smiling crew member yelled after them and the other tourists as they disembarked. They'd been given detailed instructions about what was acceptable with regard to interacting with the animals.

After spending most of the day lying in a lounge chair and struggling with a paperback that wasn't holding her interest, Eva was happy to finally be up and about. The idea had been to avoid awkward time alone with Rafe. Not that she'd had any kind of success with that goal—she hadn't been able to stop thinking about him.

The way he'd moved to the music last night, how he'd held her in his arms… The intensity of his darkened, heated gaze on hers as they'd danced the tango.

The whole day had felt like scenes from some

kind of dream or a romantic movie. Quite a fanciful thought—one she couldn't entertain right now. Her head wasn't in the right place, and she could hardly process her emotions.

She wasn't naive enough to think they could avoid addressing what was happening between them much longer, but it made more sense to do it back home. Playing tourist at a romantic, tropical resort full of adoring couples who couldn't seem to keep their hands off each other was an all-too-tempting environment. They were even sharing the same suite, for heaven's sake.

She'd have a much clearer head back in Puerto Rico. Or maybe she was just procrastinating because she had no idea how to even start such a conversation. What would she even say?

Hey, boss. So I think maybe we should try and cool it a bit and not act like hormonal teenagers who have a crush on each other.

"The sign says we're likely to see some iguanas that way," Rafe said, pulling her out of her thoughts. She'd been absentmindedly following him down a sandy path toward the center of the island. The other tourists seemed to have dispersed in myriad other directions.

"Or we could head the other way, where there's supposed to be some large African violet bush that houses several species of exotic birds."

"I say we start with lizards," she answered. Not a phrase she'd have anticipated saying before today. In fact, there were a lot of things happening to her she wouldn't have anticipated.

Rafe nodded, then stepped the other way. "Lizards it is."

They'd ventured a couple of yards or so when a black-and-white ball of fur darted in front of them and under a bush a few feet away. Startled, Eva clasped a hand to her chest. "What was that?"

"Not a lizard," Rafe answered. "Unless the Bahamian ones have fur."

A low mewing noise sounded from the bush the furball had run under. "Do you hear that?" Eva asked, straining her ears. "It sounds like a cat."

Rafe rubbed his chin. "What would a cat be doing here? I doubt felines are one of the rare indigenous creatures inhabiting this island."

"I don't know. I suppose it must have stowed away on one of the boats and then gotten stuck here."

The mewing seemed to grow louder. "We can't just leave it here, can we?" Rafe asked.

She wouldn't even entertain the thought. A kitten didn't belong alone on an isolated island full of wild creatures who may hurt it. Or worse. "Absolutely not."

"Huh. Let's go tell the crew, then. Maybe they can send someone out to fetch it and take it back to an animal shelter on the main island."

That sounded like as good a plan as any. Before they turned to do just that, the little creature darted out once more and ran farther away, deeper into the rough. Despite moving rather fast, Eva could tell it was limping drastically on one side, which would explain the mewing cries. "I think it's hurt," she said, following the little paw prints in the sand. "The poor thing."

"I wonder how long it's been here."

Eva felt a rush of tears to her eyes. "She must be in pain. And so scared."

"I'll bet it's starving, too."

They followed the sound of mews until they reached yet another bush. A large insect jumped across Eva's foot and she bit back a startled yelp. "We can't just keep chasing it. We might be making its injury worse."

"I don't suppose you have anything that might lure her out?"

Eva reached into her dress pocket. "You're a genius!"

Rafe tossed her a pleased smile. "I am?"

"Yes!" she declared, pulling out what she'd been carrying next to her cell phone. "Because you reminded me of this. As luck would have it, I grabbed a granola bar from one of the breakfast buffets because I wasn't sure how long this tour would be." She flashed him the granola bar.

"I'd say the genius is the person who happens to have food in her pocket."

Or maybe they just made a good team, Eva thought—though she would keep that thought to herself.

It took some coaxing, and a trail of granola bits thrown its way, but the cat slowly made its way to them. Eva deftly managed to pick the animal up without spooking it while it was distracted by the food. She stood with it cradled in her arms.

She immediately saw what had the poor animal in such distress. Several sharp burrs had dug into its two hind legs.

"Help me hold her steady?" she said to Rafe. He immediately complied and she cautiously removed each offending burr. For her efforts, she was gifted with a few swipes of needle-sharp claws. But the poor thing was too weak to do more than scratch the surface of Eva's skin.

Finally, when Eva had removed the last sharp prick, the cat mewed softly, then set its head down on her forearm.

"How ironic that someone named Gato would be rescuing a cat," Rafe commented.

That was rather amusing. "Perhaps it's fate,

predestined," Eva speculated. "I've never rescued one before, or anything else for that matter."

"Let's see if we can get this little one on the boat and then back to civilization."

Gingerly, she stepped out of the shrubbery and started heading toward the beach. Rafe stopped her with a hand on her shoulder. "That's not the right way."

"Are you sure?"

He glanced over his shoulder. Then past hers. "I guess not entirely."

It appeared they were lost. After several false starts, they finally determined the right path and started walking back to the shore.

But when they got to the dock where the boat had been, it was completely empty.

Rafe swore. "I don't believe this. Looks like they all left. We must have been gone longer than we thought."

Eva maneuvered around the animal in her arms to click on her cell phone. Her heart sank when she saw the screen. "I have no signal."

Rafe quickly scanned his own phone. "Neither do I."

Her heart pounded in her chest. This couldn't be happening. "So now what?"

Rafe rubbed a hand down his face. "Maybe

we can catch a cell tower signal farther into the water."

Rafe kicked his shoes off and ventured several feet into the ocean. Even from this distance, Eva could tell from his expression that he was having no luck. When he came back to her side, he was soaked up to his waist.

"Any thoughts of a plan B?" she asked, the trepidation now cresting into a full peak in her chest.

Rafe shoved his phone into his now wet pocket. "Well, Paolo said the tours come daily. Worst case scenario, we're here until the next one arrives tomorrow."

Blood rushed out of her face at the thought of being stranded. "That's a pretty bad scenario."

"Maybe there are other resorts who send guests here." Although Rafe didn't sound convinced, Eva decided she would latch on to that possibility—and fervently hoped it was a feasible one.

She was stranded on an island with a man she'd been trying to avoid being alone with. If the scenario weren't so dire, it would have made her laugh.

This couldn't really be happening. How had he ended up in what could be a scene out of an adventure movie? Rafe powered off his phone and reset it for what had to be the dozenth time.

"Anything?" Eva asked, studying the device. The cat still slept, curled up in her arms. As happy as Rafe was that they'd rescued the poor thing, the silly castaway was the reason they were in this mess.

Stranded on an island. It was almost comical. If it weren't so dire.

"Not a single bar," he answered Eva, slamming the phone back into his pants pocket.

"I don't understand how they could have just left us here."

"Paolo said he was going to call to add us to the manifest. I'm guessing it was so last minute no one informed the crew member in charge of head count."

"Maybe they'll figure it out and come back for us," Eva stated. The words sounded like a plea to the universe.

"Maybe," he agreed, though he didn't believe it for a second. Most likely, everyone was off the boat and on to thinking about their dinner plans by now.

He and Eva needed some kind of plan. They couldn't just stand here lamenting their luck. Plus, Eva was clearly agitated, her breath coming in gasps, her voice sounding pitchy and strained. She was panicking. They had to expend some of her nervous energy.

"Let's walk around the perimeter of the beach," he suggested. "Maybe we'll see a sailboat or someone out deep-sea fishing."

She nodded. "Good idea."

He sure hoped so, though it was a risky one. Being so far from the dock meant they might miss the boat if it did happen to come back for them. But he really didn't want to split up. The idea of leaving Eva alone on the beach didn't sit right, not in her agitated state.

They strode in silence for several minutes right on the edge of the water, the cat still cradled in Eva's arms, but nothing appeared on the horizon, not so much as a sailboat.

They'd been walking for close to ninety minutes when Rafe finally decided he had to admit the inevitable. The sky was growing darker, the possibility of any other boats arriving growing dimmer.

"How can the waters be so empty?" Eva asked, as if reading his thoughts.

"Maybe it's just our luck."

As if he'd tempted fate with his words, a massive storm cloud seemed to appear out of nowhere above them in the sky. Strong gusts of wind blew from every direction. Eva's dress skirt whipped around her legs. The kitten in her arms stirred at the disturbance.

That settled it. Some deity above was most definitely toying with them.

"You've got to be kidding me." Eva groaned. "This cannot possibly get worse."

A fat raindrop landed on her nose before she got the last word out. It was followed by several more. The cat let out an outraged meow as a few landed on her dark fur.

"We have to find shelter," he told her. "Follow me."

They'd seen a small cave during their quest for the kitten earlier. Not ideal, but at least it would provide a roof over their heads. Otherwise, they were about to be drenched and left dodging flying sand and other debris.

He could only hope a pack of lizards didn't have the same idea to take shelter there.

Eva fell in step behind him and within moments he'd located the dark opening. He sensed Eva's steps faltering behind him before they'd reached the mouth of the cave.

"What's the matter?" He turned to ask over his shoulder.

"Uh, is it safe in there?"

"Safe?"

"Like…is it empty?"

Rafe pinched the bridge of his nose. The cave

was safer than being out here. Still, he couldn't exactly blame her for being apprehensive. The opening looked ebony dark. "I'll go check it out first."

She nodded, her eyes filling with gratitude. "Thank you."

A cursory investigation a few feet in told him the cave was empty enough, sparing a few earthworms that moved out of the way when he stepped in. He motioned for Eva to come in after him.

She gingerly stepped inside, still cradling the cat, who seemed all too comfortable in Eva's arms.

"Well, it's not the Ritz," he said, striving for a light tone. "But it's a hole with a roof."

"A very dark hole," Eva said, eyes glistening in the darkness.

He fished his phone out of his pocket, called up the flashlight feature and clicked on it. A circular ray of light illuminated a small area around them. "No service but it's good for this, at least."

"Do you think there are bats in here?" she asked, her voice tight with apprehension.

Most certainly, Rafe thought. Eva had to know it, too. She was aiming for denial. "I don't know," he lied. "If there are, I'm sure they're much deeper into the depths. We're barely inside."

The tension in her face muscles seemed to relax just a bit. "I'm good with most animals. Just not bats. They give me the heebie-jeebies."

He had to smile at that. "The heebie-jeebies, huh?" Speaking of animals, she had to be tired of holding the one currently glued to her middle. "Here, let me take the cat for a bit."

She gently handed the animal over. The cat lifted a small paw in protest at the change, but then seemed to give in and settled against his chest. With one hand, he helped Eva lower herself to a seated position against the wall.

"Nothing to do but wait it out, I guess." She leaned her head back, then closed her eyes. The soft white light cast shadows over her features: regal jawline, soft nose, long, dark lashes. She had a dark smudge of dirt on her right cheek, and her hair had come loose out of its bun and fallen wildly over her face and shoulders. She was utterly stunning.

"I hope it stops soon," Eva said in a weary whisper, her eyes remaining closed. She looked utterly exhausted. Rafe's heart tugged in his chest. How had he let them fall into such a ridiculous predicament? He should have told Eva they needed to get back to the boat to have a crew member find the feral cat. If he'd only done that one simple thing, they'd be nice and warm and dry right now back at their suite. Hindsight and all that.

Rafe settled in next to Eva against the wall. "I'm guessing it's a flash storm that came out of nowhere and will probably be gone just as fast." Another lie. The commotion outside showed no sign of letting up.

Not anytime soon.

CHAPTER ELEVEN

How in the world had she ended up here? Eva shifted her weight in an effort to get more comfortable against the hard rock wall. To no avail. There was no way to make any of this more comfortable.

Her world had somehow turned to utter chaos when she hadn't been paying attention. It had only taken a few short years. She'd once been so proud of herself and all that the future held for her. School had come almost too easily. She'd gotten stellar grades and been a star with her professors. The only career she'd ever wanted was there waiting for her upon graduation. She'd had so much that she'd taken for granted: a beautiful home, a doting father, a loving sibling and a devoted friend in Fran. It had been almost perfect.

Aside from the trauma of her mother leaving, she'd led a picture-perfect life. And somehow it had all come crumbling down and she'd ended up here—shivering and wet in a dark cave with no clear idea as to when she'd be able to get out and back to civilization.

Eva felt tears of frustration and sadness sting her eyes and she fought them back. Crying wouldn't do her any good. It hadn't so far.

She had no idea how long she and Rafe had been in the cave. They simply sat in the quiet, neither one speaking a word. Finally, Rafe broke the silence.

Rafe leaned over the cat in his lap to pick up the phone on the ground next to his leg. "I hate to do this, but we should really turn the flashlight off. We might need it later and can't risk it running out of battery."

"All right."

The world went completely dark when he shut it off. Only the sound of the pounding rain and harsh wind outside filled the air, along with a gentle, soft purring that somehow served to soothe her nerves a little. How could the kitten be sleeping through all this? Probably due to the relief of finally being free of the painful burrs. She didn't regret helping the poor creature. Of course she didn't. Eva just wished she'd thought of a different way to do so.

A bolt of lightning flashed outside, lighting up the sky and her view out of the cave. The scene outside the opening looked like something out of a gothic movie, right before it all went pitch-black again a split second later. The ocean had appeared like ebony ink in the distance. The shrubbery just outside looked dark and eerie. A shiver ran down her spine.

"Are you cold?" Rafe asked, mistaking her shudder. Without waiting for an answer, he shifted closer to her and wrapped an arm around her shoulders.

Though she hadn't felt chilled, the warmth of his body sent a wave of soothing comfort through her skin. Reflexively, she nestled in closer to his length.

"I'm so sorry, Rafe," she said with a deep sigh.

"What are you apologizing for?"

He had to ask?

"Isn't it obvious? I'm the one who chased after a cat, getting us lost in the process, then sat with her until our ride back to civilization left us behind. This is all my fault." The laugh out of her that followed sounded nearly maniacal to her own ears. How many times had she uttered that phrase lately?

"I'd like you to try and get those words out of your vernacular, Eva. Just try."

"How can you deny that my actions led to us being here?" she demanded. Her voice sounded harsh, though she realized how unreasonable that was. Rafe was simply being kind.

Rafe gave her shoulder a squeeze. "We're equally culpable."

She grunted a chuckle. "How do you figure that?"

He shrugged against her. "I was just thinking how all I had to do was suggest we go back to the boat to notify someone that there was a domestic animal on the island that clearly didn't belong here. I followed our little pal just the same way you did."

"As if I gave you a chance to do anything else."

"Last I checked I had free will. I was perfectly capable back then of telling you no."

"That seems to be my problem. No one ever seems to tell me no. Or that I've messed up." Something about sitting in the dark must have loosened her tongue. She'd had no idea she was going to utter those words until they were out of her mouth.

"You think that's a problem?"

"I'm saying it's a double-edged sword."

"I think you've gotten too used to swallowing blame. Guilt is almost second nature to you now, isn't it? Because of one bad move you made."

"It was a disastrous move, Rafe. A calamity that led to other calamities."

"I agree."

His answer surprised her for its bluntness. "You do?"

"Yep. You experienced the type of betrayal most people would never recover from. They might become bitter and angry for years after. Maybe forever."

Ah, so that was his angle. A dose of reverse psychology. She wasn't going to fall for it. "I'd say they'd have every right." As would she.

He rested his head back against the wall, Eva sensing and hearing the motion more than she could make out anything in the dark. "Maybe. But it would be a terrible way to live. A waste of life."

She supposed he had a point. But she was in no mood to entertain it at the moment—or to tell him that he might be right.

Rafe spoke again. "You mentioned no one told you no, that your father and brother were forgiving and understanding through it all."

"That's right." The same way Rafe was being now, about the fact they were stranded on an island as a direct result of her impromptu decisions.

"Have you ever thought of forgiving yourself?" he asked, his voiced drifting to her in the dark.

The question rattled her.

"The way your father and brother have?" Rafe added.

Of course, she'd thought about it—wished there was some way that she might. The effort had been futile, beyond reach.

"I don't think I can."

"Why?" He sounded utterly exasperated.

"Not until I've made some kind of restitution or figured out a way to undo the damage my actions caused."

"Like what?"

She honestly didn't know. Not that she hadn't racked her brain trying to come up with a solution. "That's the question, isn't it?" The obvious answer was to get the distillery back somehow. But it belonged to Rafe now. There was no way she could afford a repurchase. Not without a miracle.

"Look," Rafe began. He sounded like he was about to try a different tactic, as the last one had clearly fallen flat. "As someone who's never been given any kind of grace throughout any part of his life, my suggestion is that you do your best to try and move on and appreciate the way your father and brother love you. Trust me."

His words gave her pause—not so much his advice, but the first part of what he'd said. *Never been given any kind of grace.*

Eva had been sitting here, doing what she so often did—focusing on herself and what she'd been going through. What exactly was Rafe's story?

She'd been telling herself she didn't want to push. But it occurred to her that maybe she should have.

"Tell me." She reached for his arm, took his hand in hers. "I want to hear it, Rafe."

Rafe felt his muscles tighten up at Eva's prompt. The poor animal in his lap must have sensed the tension in his muscles as it stirred with a stretch, then moved over to settle on top of Eva's thighs.

"I want to hear whatever you're ready to tell me," she repeated. The words nudged him toward a trip down memory lane he wasn't sure he was ready to take—a trip he'd been avoiding for as long as he could.

"What happened that night in Seattle?" Eva's voice was barely more than a whisper.

His heart hammered in his chest. Sitting here in the dark, with her delicate yet strong hand holding tight to his, a part of him wanted nothing more than to vent all of it. Just let it go once and for all.

An equally strong part of him wanted it buried deep and well in the past where it belonged.

Except it wasn't really fully submerged there, was it? Not judging by the way a layer of sweat had formed on his forehead.

He took a deep breath, trying to figure out how to begin in such a way that he might shut the conversation down if it became too much. The pitch-black of the darkness helped.

He released a deep sigh. "The same thing that had been happening for years. Only this time I reacted."

Eva gave his hand a reassuring squeeze, silent encouragement to continue.

"The one time I didn't walk away."

"How so?"

The answer to that question was where his thoughts got all jumbled up. What had gone down that day had started years earlier—scab after scab that had been repeatedly picked at, leaving countless scars.

"I ran into someone from my past that night. It didn't go well."

"Your past?"

Maybe it was the complete darkness, or maybe it was simply the way Eva was holding his hand, but his mind didn't immediately shut down at the thought of getting into the telling of that night the way it usually did.

"I didn't have a lot growing up," he began, grasping for the right words. "It was just me and my mom. She resented me. I sensed it before I was old enough to form coherent thoughts."

He heard her suck in a breath. Though his mouth had gone dry, he made himself continue. "My mom stuck around, but we both might have been better off if she hadn't. The older I got, the colder she became. For her, a preteen son meant nothing but responsibility and another mouth to feed."

"Oh, Rafe." Eva's voice held no trace of pity, just understanding and sympathy. She had no idea how much that meant.

"So I did my best to stay out of her way," he continued. "Studied a lot. Stayed after school to use the computer lab. Went to the library on the weekends to use the computers there."

"You must have been so lonely."

He hadn't realized it then, hadn't felt alone. And compared to what had come next in his life, the solitude had been a blessing.

"The hard work paid off." In one sense, anyway. "A teacher noticed I had a gift, as he called it. He helped me to reach out to a prestigious boarding school outside of Seattle. I got in with a full scholarship."

"That sounds like quite an accomplishment."

"It was the beginning of a nightmare. I tried to leave more than once. But whenever I asked to come back home, my mom immediately shut it down. She finally had her freedom and didn't want me around. For months, I couldn't even reach her." He drew a breath deep into his lungs. "She didn't return my calls."

"Oh, no," Eva said on a soft whisper.

"I didn't fit in at Brimford Boarding School for Young Men. The other boys made sure to remind me in frequent and often humiliating ways just how much I did not belong there with them."

Thoughts rushed through his mind of the frequent beatings he'd taken, the humiliating shoves for simply walking down the hallway to class. The laptop he'd had to learn to fix after it had been pulled out of his hands and thrown into a nearby bush. The sneers and taunts that made fun of his clothes, his hair, his very self.

"What did they do?"

"I wasn't a terribly bulky teenager. In fact, I was downright scrawny by comparison. I hadn't reached a growth spurt yet."

He heard her sniffle and hoped she wasn't crying for him, because he couldn't bear that.

"I survived it, obviously, graduated and got into Berkeley, again with a full scholarship. Then I developed the productivity app that was successful beyond my wildest dreams. So I did my best to put it all behind me. Until about a decade later, when I ran into one of my old classmates. And then it was as if nothing had changed."

Eva's heart was slowly splintering in her chest for the boy Rafe had been, and all the obstacles he'd had to overcome to become the highly successful man he was now. How different their childhoods had been. Eva had always enjoyed the bastion of love so freely lavished on her by her family—Nana's maternal comfort, Papá's quiet yet fierce affection, Teo's brotherly protectiveness.

Rafe hadn't enjoyed anything remotely similar.

He'd been silent for several moments now, only the sound of his breathing echoing through the darkness. She waited patiently, willing him to continue for both their sakes. She'd bet her next breath that he needed to get some of this out and off his chest. For her, she desperately wanted to understand him better, to learn more about what he'd endured to get to where he was as the accomplished tech tycoon who'd come so far from his origins.

Just as she considered how to give him a little nudge, Rafe slowly began speaking again.

"Trina convinced me to go out that night. Wanted to be seen at the newest dance club that was opening to VIPs only that evening. Clubbing is one of my least favorite things to do."

Eva hadn't missed the "to be seen" part of his statement. An interesting side note.

Rafe continued. "But that night I decided I liked arguing with her even less than going out. So I agreed." He sucked in a breath before going on. "A few minutes after we got there, I heard a loud, familiar voice call my name from behind, just as a heavy hand fell on my shoulder."

A knot of apprehension twisted in Eva's middle.

"I recognized him immediately despite the years since I'd seen him last: someone I'd gone to school with. A senior who'd been particularly cruel."

Eva could guess what had happened next.

"He acted like we were long-lost buddies or something. Talked about how he'd been reading about my successes over the years."

Bingo. She'd been right.

"I tried to brush him off, wanted nothing to do with his fake memories. He'd made my life a daily hell and now he wanted to pretend we were simply old school chums."

"What happened next?"

"He became hostile immediately. He made derogatory comments about how I might have fooled everyone but he knew who I really was. I tried to walk away. I really did." She heard him take a shaky breath. "But as soon as I turned I felt a forceful shove that nearly sent me to the floor. Just like back at school."

"Oh, Rafe."

"And then something I can't even describe just came over me. I couldn't take it one more second, not one more thing. I turned back around and threw the first punch—hard enough that I heard his jaw crack. I knew I'd broken it."

The brute had had it coming, more than deserved a punch and worse. But Eva kept the thought to herself and let Rafe continue.

"He had others with him who quickly became involved. Someone decided they were on my side and jumped. Before I knew it, the altercation had grown. Several more club goers became involved until it was some kind of crowd riot. By the time the authorities showed up, the place was a mess."

"Oh, my," Eva whispered. She'd read various reports but hadn't looked into the details. Those gossip sites weren't ones she visited; she hardly considered them credible.

Rafe went on. "I awoke the next morning with a cut lip and a bruised face and a heart full of remorse. Then there were all the tabloid headlines online. They all read something to the effect that it was no wonder given my background and where I came from. Such behavior was hardly surprising given my upbringing. Someone started a rumor that I might have stolen the app idea, that a man like me couldn't have come up with it and developed it myself. It all became too much. I had no place in my own life."

Eva supplied the rest. "So you walked away from it all to become a rum distiller in Puerto Rico."

She felt him nod next to her. "That's right. I paid the establishment for damages, covered the cost of medical bills for anyone who was injured and completed a short probationary penalty. Then I began to pack. You know the rest."

Eva took a moment to process all that she'd just been told. It was a wonder the man hadn't rebuffed all of humanity and gone off to become a hermit somewhere. She was about to tell him how much his resilience and strength impressed her when Rafe surprised her with his next words.

"I'm just sorry my newfound life came at such a personal cost to you, Eva."

Eva sucked in a breath. "I did that to myself, Rafe. If you hadn't bought Gato Rums, someone else would have." That was the absolute truth.

She felt him squeeze her hand before he let it go. "I will say that I'm not sorry I made the purchase. Because otherwise, I would have never met you."

Eva couldn't help the small chuckle that escaped her. "Yeah? Well, you also wouldn't be stranded on an island in the middle of a violent tropical storm stuck in a cave."

Rafe didn't laugh in response. "Small price to pay."

CHAPTER TWELVE

A PAIR OF reptilian eyes were staring into his.

Rafe awoke with a start and tried hard to focus on his surroundings. It took a moment to recollect where he was. He and Eva had spent the night in the cave, and a large iguana had decided to share their space at some point.

A glance outside told him it was light out. Shockingly, they must have fallen asleep and stayed that way till morning. He had no clue what time it might be.

He used his foot to gently shoo the creature away. It swiveled its head in disgust but slowly started to saunter out of the opening. It appeared their rescue feline wasn't any kind of guard cat.

What he discovered next was almost as alarming as waking up to a lizard—Eva sat cradled in his lap. A vague recollection of her yelping in discomfort in the middle of the night surfaced in his mind. He remembered lifting her onto his thighs in an effort to make her more comfortable. Luckily, she was still asleep now as he pondered what to do about the predicament.

He was trying to figure out a gentle way to shift her from his lap when her eyes fluttered open. "Rafe?" Her voice sounded gravelly, full of sleep.

"Good morning, sweetheart."

Her gaze traveled to the opening, then filled with surprise. "I can't believe we were here all night."

Rafe watched her eyes widen as she registered exactly where and how she was sitting. But she made no effort to move. And he made no effort to let go of her. In fact, his hands seemed to move of their own volition and he grasped her tighter around the waist. And then the world seemed to stop, for Eva had moved to straddle him, her eyes clouded with desire. A searing need shot through him at the intimate contact.

"Rafe?" she repeated. His name on her lips only served to spike his desire. She was asking an entirely different question this time, and he was all too eager to answer it.

He thrust his hands into her hair, then pulled her head closer. But then he waited; the next move had to be hers. Her lips found his a moment later and he was mindless with need. He wanted her, so badly he ached with need.

She devoured his mouth with her own, sending heat and longing through his core. He would never get enough of her—her taste, her scent, the soft feel of her curves in his palms.

A warning cry shouted in his mind that this was madness. Neither one of them was thinking straight…or thinking at all. But he couldn't bring himself to heed it.

Yearnings he'd fought since he'd first laid eyes on her refused to be contained any longer, though he knew it was so wrong.

Eva moaned into his mouth and it was the sweetest sound he'd ever heard. But another noise reached his ears just then—a sound that had him slowly spinning back to reality.

With great effort, he made himself pull away. "We have to stop, sweetheart."

She blinked at him in confusion and he swore silently at how strong his urge was to take her mouth once more. The sound echoed from the distance outside again. If Eva heard it, she made no indication.

Rafe swallowed, fighting to catch his breath. "We have to stop," he repeated. "I think I hear a boat."

That seemed to finally catch her attention. Eva's eyes widened and she scrambled off him, holding her lips with her fingers. She hesitated for just a moment before reality seemed to dawn in her eyes.

"We have to get out there," she announced, her voice full of panic. With haste, she reached down to cradle the sleeping cat. Rafe stood with no small amount of effort, his stiff legs crying out in pain. He reached a hand to help Eva up. She groaned as she stood on wobbly legs.

When they stepped outside, a small speedboat could be seen in the water fast approaching the beach. It appeared to be carrying two men. Rafe recognized them as Paolo and his nephew, the captain who had brought them here yesterday. Even from here he could tell the former looked furious.

"Let's go." He took Eva by the elbow, helping her through the shrubbery and then the sand.

They reached the water just as the boat reached the shore.

Paolo jumped out, his hand clasped to his chest, offering a flurry of apologies. He pointed with his thumb behind him at the other man. "My nephew is a fool who should have been more competent than to leave two guests stranded on an island."

Rafe couldn't argue with that.

"I was looking for you this morning to discuss our deal and the two of you were nowhere to be found," Paolo explained. "I realized what must have happened after speaking with the crew."

It was just as they'd suspected; they hadn't been added on to the manifest list in time and had been forgotten as a result.

"I'm just glad you're here now," Eva said behind him. She lifted the load she held to show him. "We found a stray cat and chased him to make sure he wasn't left behind again. So it's partly our doing that we missed the boat."

Rafe bit back a retort at her statement. This wasn't the time to point it out, but the woman was practically apologizing for having been deserted, for heaven's sake.

The captain ducked his head, mumbling an apology of his own.

"How can we ever make this up to you?" Paolo asked, his tone full of remorse.

"Just get us back to the island," Rafe answered, taking Eva by the hand and helping her onboard.

The engine roared to life and they circled around. Eva sat next to him staring out at the horizon. The cat stretched and yawned in her arms, apparently not bothered by the motion of the boat.

Rafe swore under his breath. There was no way to deny any longer what was clearly happening between them—though now that they were headed back to the main island and back to reality, the folly of losing control the way he had back at the cave became undeniably clear. There was no question that he would have made love to her if the boat hadn't arrived when it did. He'd lost control both then and the night before when he'd overshared, telling her so much about Seattle and his life before.

And there was no way he could take any of it back.

It was hard to wrap her head around what had happened over the past twelve hours. Eva watched from her perch starboard as the main island came into view. Fran wasn't going to believe any of this when she told her.

Her phone immediately started buzzing as soon as they got within range. Eva was too tired and too emotionally drained to even check the screen. Whatever it was it could wait. She could still taste Rafe on her lips, and her body still felt heated where his hands had touched her skin.

A flush crept into her cheeks and she uttered a silent prayer of gratitude that it was too windy to notice—not that Rafe was so much as looking in her direction. He seemed just as wrapped up in his thoughts as she was.

When they disembarked on the dock moments later, her phone vibrated in her pocket once more.

She handed Paolo the cat. He assured them he'd bring it to a local veterinarian to be checked out and then to a shelter. A pang of loss swept through her as she handed the animal over. But she hardly had the mental nor physical room in her life right now for a pet.

Finally pulling the gadget out, she frowned at the screen.

"Everything all right?" Rafe asked as they made their way down the pathway leading to their suite.

"I'm not sure. Looks like everyone but Teo has left me messages. There's some from Nana, Fran and my father."

"That's curious," Rafe offered, though he sounded distracted. Eva could hardly blame him for not being hyper-focused on her at the moment. They'd been through quite an ordeal.

"I'll call them as soon as I can think straight," she told him. "Which isn't remotely likely to happen until I can take a shower and find some caffeine."

The rest of the walk followed in awkward silence. Eva released a sigh of relief when they finally reached the suite. She shut her room's door, then leaned against it to catch her breath.

Her phone vibrated again.

The screen popped up with the contact photo of her father. With a resigned sigh, Eva unlocked it and clicked on the icon. After what she'd done to the man, the least she could do was answer his phone call.

"Hola, Papá," she began. "I'm sorry I missed your calls. You wouldn't believe—"

But he cut her off before she could explain. What he told her turned her blood to ice.

Did she think less of him now? Rafe braced his palms against the tile wall of the shower and let the hot spray wash over him. The water felt welcome and soothing on his sore muscles but inside he still felt raw and bruised. He never talked to anyone about his past. For some reason, he'd poured out his soul to a woman who worked for him.

A mocking voice sounded in his head. That was a ridiculous way to describe Eva. She was so much more to him now than any employee. Even before the heated moment of passion, he'd grown to feel emotions and longings for her he'd never felt before. Too bad the timing and circumstances were so wrong. Rafe had no clear idea of who he was and what he wanted. He had no one in his life he was close to, no one he could so much as call a friend, other than his former secretary. What could a man like that offer a woman like Eva? Not much. She needed so much more in life than a loner who hadn't been able to establish even one close in every environment he'd ever found himself in. She'd been burned too badly before by her ex-husband. He didn't need to add any more turmoil to her life.

So what was he going to do about it?

With no easy or clear answers, he shut off the water in disgust and stepped out. He'd just toweled off and thrown a pair of shorts on when the sudden noise of loud knocking sounded at the door. He bit out a curse, not ready to deal with anyone or anything right now. All he wanted was a strong cup of coffee and to put his feet up until he regained some more blood circulation through his legs.

The knock sounded again.

Sighing, he walked over to the door and pulled it open. Eva stood on the other side. She was ghostly pale and visibly shaking. The urge to pull her into his arms was immediate and strong, whatever her anguish. He fisted his hands at his side instead.

"Eva? What's wrong? Has something happened?"

She nodded, tears flooding her eyes. "Yes. It's Teo. He's been in an accident."

Rafe felt his jaw fall open in shock and concern.

"I don't have the details," Eva continued, her voice shaky. "But I have to get back home right away. I have to get back to Puerto Rico as soon as possible."

Rafe did take hold of her then, embracing her tightly until the trembling slightly lessened, as if he could somehow absorb all her dismay. "Leave it to me," he said against her ear. "I'll take care of everything and get us back right away. Go pack your things."

She hiccupped a thank-you, then fled back to her room. Rafe absentmindedly found a shirt and threw it on. Then he started making phone calls.

They were on the runway about to take off in a private jet an hour after Eva had first knocked on Rafe's door. She had so much to thank him for. He'd arranged for a flight and even helped her with her packing. Right now, he sat in the seat next to her, holding tightly to her hand, simply offering the emotional crutch she so badly needed.

"You said Teo was in an accident," Rafe said as they taxied. "What happened?"

Eva closed her eyes, a shudder racking through her whole body. "A car accident. He's shattered his leg and hasn't woken since they took him in."

"Oh, my God, Eva. I'm so sorry, sweetheart."

She wanted so badly to shut down, to just switch off her emotions until they reached Puerto Rico, where she would have no choice but to confront all her fears. But she didn't deserve that luxury. She had to get this out, had to tell someone what she suspected. "My father said he was in Cordaro. There's an international raceway there. Papá said Teo was racing one of his cars."

Rafe lifted an eyebrow. "I thought he just collected and worked on cars. I didn't realize he raced them himself."

Guilt washed over her before she could answer. "He didn't. Not until now."

"What made him start?"

She groaned aloud as the tears flooded her eyes. "I think it was because of me."

Rafe turned to face her fully. "I don't understand."

Eva gripped his hand tighter, trying to absorb some of his strength and comfort. "Teo said something to me back at the hacienda, that first night after you arrived. He said that if I really wanted to buy the distillery back, that he would find a way to help me. I think that's what he was doing."

"How?"

"Apparently, it was a private event held by

some hotshot businessman who offered a large cash prize. Teo must have entered. Then he crashed." The horror of her words threatened to overwhelm her, but she made herself continue. "And he did it because he wanted me to have the money."

"Eva, you can't believe that."

She did, because it was the only explanation that made sense. "I wish I'd never laid eyes on that man," she said, full of anguish and misery. Rafe could have no doubt who she was referring to.

Rafe released a deep sigh. "You couldn't help who you fell in love with, Eva."

Eva sucked in a breath, gathering her thoughts. "That's just it. What Victor and I had wasn't love. Deep in my soul I knew it. Real love wouldn't have asked so much of me until there was hardly anything left."

"What do you mean?"

Eva sucked in a much-needed breath, gathering the words she wanted to say. He had shared so much with her last night. Would it be so bad for her to share a little bit herself now?

She pushed ahead. "I was convinced there was something missing in my life when I met Victor," she confided. "I didn't even know what. But as much as I loved the hacienda and living on the island, I was yearning for some kind of excitement. Something different."

"Enter your ex," Rafe supplied.

She could only nod. "He seemed perfect, appearing at the perfect time." She paused until she could pull herself together a bit more. "People warned me about him. Everybody did. Fran, being such a close friend, was the most vocal."

"You had to find out for yourself. You know you did."

She immediately shook her head in protest. Rafe was just being kind, saying the things he thought would make her feel better. But she knew the truth: her brother was in a coma with a damaged limb and Eva was the one who'd indirectly put him there. "I refused to see what was right in front of me."

"What was that? At first, I mean."

"He made me feel so special. Like I was the only person that mattered. He told me I was beautiful and smart and accomplished. All the while he was plotting. In the meantime, he grew manipulative."

Rafe remained quiet, giving her all the time she needed to get this out in her own way.

Eva inhaled a shaky breath, the memories searing so painfully through her she thought she might burst. "The compliments eventually grew few and far between, until eventually I seemed to be able to do nothing right in his eyes."

Rafe still didn't speak, just let out a low whistle of a breath.

"It was almost habitual, then. My daily mission became trying to ensure he was happy with me, that I'd pleased him."

The stinging behind her eyes had grown into a burning sensation now. She wiped away a tear before it could fall. "If I didn't agree to something he'd suggested right away, even something as simple as what to have for dinner, his entire demeanor became hostile and vindictive."

Eva saw Rafe's other hand curl into a tight fist. "Did he...?"

She immediately shook her head before he could ask the question. "No, he never became physical." Though she had no confidence whatsoever that he wouldn't have—given enough time. Thank God she would never have to find out.

She went on. "Eventually, it became so hard just to get through the day. Every thought I had was consumed with what I could do to make my husband happy with me. Then I would just try harder when things inevitably went sour again. It was a vicious cycle that kept repeating."

"He tormented you," Rafe bit out.

"I let it happen. I wasn't strong enough to see it or stop it."

Rafe leaned toward her, then cupped her chin with his hand. "Men like him are good at what they do, Eva. Tell me the rest," he prompted.

"I'm not sure how or when it happened. But one day I woke up and decided I just wasn't going to do it anymore. I pushed back when he insulted me. Countered with my own opinion when I didn't agree with something he'd said or done. I think that's when he decided he would leave. His reign of influence was coming to an end, and he must have sensed it." She puffed out a breath. "But by then it was too late. So much damage had been done."

"But not to your soul, Eva. He never managed to crush it."

"How can you say that?" She forced out the question, her voice shaking.

"The fact that he manipulated you has nothing to do with how strong you are. You were taken advantage of. And you didn't let it continue. You pushed back, eventually."

Eva tried to grasp at his words, to take them to heart. But the effort was futile. Maybe someday she'd see reason behind all that Rafe was trying to tell her…but not today.

So she did the only other thing she could think of. She leaned into him, letting the tears fall freely now. He simply held her without saying a word.

Offering her so much more than she deserved.

CHAPTER THIRTEEN

RAFE STUDIED EVA as they rode the elevator to the fourth floor of the San Paolo Clinicia in Cordaro, Puerto Rico. She was spent. Dark circles framed her swollen, red eyes and her lips were drawn tight, her skin a faint shade of her normal color.

Anger still beat like a jackhammer in his chest. It had started on the jet as she'd been speaking of her ex.

Maybe all the tabloids were right. Maybe he was a brute with a violent past from the wrong side of the Seattle streets. Because he didn't think he could restrain himself if he ever came across the man who had caused Eva so much pain, when all she'd done was fall in love with him.

How could anyone be fool enough not to realize how fortunate that made them?

He wished there was a way to wipe his entire existence from Eva's memory, to replace it with peace and tranquility. He'd give anything to free her of the pain and anguish she was in right now.

The elevator dinged when they reached their floor and Eva stepped to the doors before they'd even slid open. She rushed out in a flash, jogging down the hallway until she reached the room they'd been told housed her brother. Rafe was a step behind her, and he entered to find her in a tight embrace with her grandmother. A man he recognized as her father stood by his son's bedside. Teo looked bruised and battered; Rafe hardly recognized him against the sterile white sheets of the hospital bed.

Eva rushed to her father next, then took her brother's hand and brushed a kiss on his cheek. Even from the doorway, Rafe could see the tears streaming down her cheeks.

Rafe stepped away, feeling awkward and out of place. He found a chair down the hall and took a seat. The Gatos didn't need the presence of a stranger right now. They needed each other. He was an outsider who didn't belong, just like always.

But he had no intention to leave. He would stay and wait for her in case she needed him.

He had no idea how much time had passed before a shadow fell in front of his feet and he felt her presence.

"Hey," Eva said in a raspy and strained voice.

"Hey, yourself."

She plopped into the chair next to him, releasing a long sigh. "Thank you for staying."

He simply shrugged; he wasn't about to say aloud that he couldn't imagine leaving her during such a dark hour. "You're welcome. How is he?"

"Good news," Eva answered. "I was told he was awake for a while just before we arrived. The doctor said that means he's out of the woods."

A wave of relief washed over him. He didn't know Teo well, but the brief amount of time he'd spent with the man had shown him to be warm and genuine. And if Eva was right about the cause of his accident, Teo was a generous soul who'd just risked his life to help his sister.

He reached for her, interlacing his fingers with hers. "I'm so happy to hear that."

She leaned into his shoulder. "Teo's got a long road ahead of him. His leg took the brunt of the impact. There'll be a lot of rehabilitation before he has use of it again. And he might not ever get full use back."

"I'm sorry" was all he could think to say.

Eva nodded slowly against his upper arm. "We're just so grateful to have him awake again. To know he's going to be okay."

"We'll do everything we can to make sure

he gets all the help he needs to recover as best as he can."

"Thank you, Rafe. That's if I can keep from throttling him for the scare he gave everyone."

Rafe chuckled. "Try to cut him some slack. He's been through a lot."

"I'll try." He heard her release a deep sigh. "I'm sorry we had to rush away from the resort before finalizing things," she began. "I know how much that deal meant to you."

He had to smile at that. "You really need to stop apologizing to me. Especially about something like this."

"Okay. Sorry," she said with a cheeky grin.

They sat that way for several moments, in comfortable silence. He couldn't bring himself to let go of her hand, and she made no effort to drop his.

Until he caught movement down the hall. She pulled her hand away then, placing it on her lap.

Eva's father stepped out of the room and approached them from the hallway. "Hola, Rafael," he greeted him.

"Hola, Señor Gato. I'm glad Teo will be all right."

"Thank you. It's a blessing from above." He addressed his daughter. "Why don't you two go get some rest, maybe something to eat? They're going to take Teo up for some more tests. By then visiting hours will be over and the hospital only allows two people in the patient's room after that. Nana and I will stay."

Eva didn't protest, a testament to how tired she was. "Okay, Papá."

Rafe stood to shake the man's hand. "I hope Teo has a restful night."

Señor Gato nodded with a tired smile.

"We'll be back first thing tomorrow morning," Eva told her father. "Please call with updates about how he's doing."

"I will, *mi hija*."

The two of them began walking down the hall. Eva slipped her hand back into his before they reached the elevator. Reflexively, Rafe brought it to his lips. She could cling to him for as long as she needed.

Eva waited in the lobby of a quaint one-floor hotel about three miles from the hospital. Rafe stood at the desk checking them in for the night. It had been his idea to stay close by, understanding without her having to tell him that she didn't want to be too far from her family and injured brother. The hacienda was about an hour away. Much too far.

She watched Rafe now as he spoke to the attendant. He'd really come through for her when she'd needed it the most, jetting them back home, supporting her through the panic and worry. And just listening.

Suddenly, it dawned on her just how much she needed him by her side at this moment. Yet another shock. Even though they'd only known each other a few short weeks, it had taken a near tragedy for her to realize that she wanted—no, *needed*—the strength and mental fortitude that Rafe somehow gave her. She couldn't imagine having taken that phone call from Papá without Rafe there to help her deal with the news.

That settled it. She didn't want to entertain any kind of pretense at this moment, not with everything happening. The thought of spending the night by herself alone, plagued with guilt and worry in an unfamiliar hotel room, suddenly both depressed and horrified her.

She strode to the desk before she could change her mind.

Touching Rafe on his arm, she waited until he excused himself to the attendant and turned to her.

"Everything all right, Eva? Did you change your mind and decide you'd prefer to go home?"

She shook her head. "No. If it's all right with you, I'd prefer if we shared one room." She sucked in a breath before continuing. "I'd rather not be alone tonight."

A myriad of emotions seemed to play behind his eyes. Eva couldn't guess what he might be thinking, just fervently hoped that he wouldn't turn her down. Without any further hesitation, he gave her a single nod. "Of course." He turned back to the attendant.

A few minutes later, they entered through the door of a cozy-looking and well-kept room. A flat-screen TV hung on the wall opposite the bed, while a colorful circular rug covered the hardwood floors. Cheery curtains with a colorful floral pattern hung parted on the sole window.

Rafe noticed it before she did. He swore quietly. "Sorry, Eva. I promise I asked for double beds. I'll go see about switching rooms."

Maybe it was the fact that she was just too tired to cope with any further delays, or maybe her vulnerability was too close to the surface, but she didn't want him to bother. She stopped him with a hand on his arm before he reached the door. "Let's just try and get some rest. I can barely stay upright much longer."

He lifted an eyebrow. "I can sleep on the floor."

"It's okay, Rafe. We spent the night together in an abandoned cave. I think we can handle a soft bed."

Their gazes locked with the obvious left

unspoken—the way things had turned out in said cave the next morning.

Eva didn't care. She just wanted a shower and to get some much-needed sleep.

Twenty minutes later, when she exited the bathroom, Rafe was already in bed scrolling through his phone. He'd shut his bedside lamp off.

"Good night, Rafe."

Eva crawled in next to him on the mattress. Surprisingly, the close proximity didn't make her self-conscious. In a way, it felt completely natural. She was reaching for her own lamp to turn it off when her phone dinged with a text.

She grabbed it immediately to check, heart pounding in her chest that it might be more bad news that her brother had taken a turn for the worse. Relief surged through her when she read the message.

"Anything new?" Rafe asked.

"No. No updates. Just my dad bidding us a good night."

Rafe shifted on the mattress. "I hope he and Nana manage to get some sleep. They both looked pretty spent."

"I hope so, too," Eva agreed with a sigh. "Though it's doubtful. Papá will fret all night and Nana won't leave Teo's side."

"You and Teo are lucky to have them."

Eva didn't miss the note of sorrow in Rafe's voice. She could imagine why discussing family might sadden him, given the way he'd had to grow up. He'd really had no one.

"Nana's been the only mother figure we had," Eva explained. "She's been a rock for all three of us since my mother left."

Rafe paused in the act of adjusting his pillow. "She left? I'm embarrassed to say that I just figured she was…"

Eva immediately knew what he meant. "No. She's fine. Just AWOL, so to speak. Has been for years."

He cleared his throat. "Do you want to tell me about it?"

She shrugged, then propped herself up on a pillow. "There's really nothing much to tell. Fairly common story, I guess. She left when I was about twelve. Teo was fourteen. She was born in Scotland and grew up in Switzerland. Spends her time traveling to various fashion events. She's a designer for a handbag company."

"Huh."

"She thought she could handle life on a Caribbean island after getting married, but decided after all those years that she didn't want to. She just left one day. Said she'd be in touch."

He let out a slow whistle. "Being abandoned

by your mother couldn't have been easy at that age. I'm sorry, Eva."

No, it hadn't. Not in the least. For years Eva had blamed herself, wondering what she might have done to keep her mother at home. She'd questioned all the reasons why it might have been her fault. Maybe if she'd helped out more around the house, been less sulky about doing her homework. If she'd just tried to be a better daughter... She shook a shaky breath before responding. "It wasn't at first. But eventually, the three of us adjusted. I learned to cook and helped dad out with the business. Luckily, Nana was nearby to help out." And thank God for that. Her grandmother had stepped into the maternal gap of her mother's absence without preamble or complaint.

"What about Teo? How did he take to being left behind by his mother?"

Rafe's question tore at her heart. No doubt he was thinking of his own experience as a child with a distant and uncaring mom. The truth was, Teo hadn't handled it well. The year Mama left had been the year he'd constantly been in and out of trouble—getting into fights, destroying property. He'd been angry and had lashed out at anything he could. But she couldn't begin to try and speak on her brother's behalf about how Mama's abandonment had affected him.

"I'll let him answer that in his own way," Eva told him. "You should ask him someday."

"Maybe I will," he answered.

"Papá has stayed in touch with her over the years," Eva told him. "Teo and I as well, to a much lesser extent."

"So you've had some contact, then."

She nodded slowly. "Minimally. Eventually, I just learned to accept that she wasn't going to come back and went about the business of growing up. Without her."

Despite the matter-of-fact delivery, Eva realized the conversation was churning up emotions she'd long thought dormant. She was trembling, her heart pounding in her chest. She refused to succumb to the temptation to give in to her anger. She'd long passed the angry phase and moved on to acceptance—right around the time she'd graduated high school and Mama's only response had been to send her a congratulatory card.

Rafe must have noticed her trembling. "Hey, come here," he said, gathering her in his arms. She didn't fight it, didn't even want to.

He still held her when she awoke the next morning.

What an eventful and harrowing twenty-four hours. Rafe couldn't remember the last time he'd felt so spent. Hard to even imagine how much more worn-down Eva must feel.

Last night had been…interesting. He'd simply held her in his arms until she'd fallen asleep. In the middle of the night, when he'd heard her sniffling and softly hiccupping in a clear sob, he'd simply pulled her closer, no words spoken. He'd just wanted her to know he was there.

He studied her profile as they were driven back to the hospital. Her features were set, her chin lifted in quiet strength.

Pity that she had no idea just how strong she was.

When they pulled up to the hospital entrance, a familiar figure bolted from the other end of the street toward the sliding doors. A smile spread across Eva's face and she hurriedly shoved her car door open before they'd even come to a full stop.

"Fran!" she shouted, jumping out of the vehicle.

So that's who that was. But Fran must not have heard her name being called because she rushed through the doors. They could see her in a near jog to the elevator.

"She really seems to be in a hurry," Rafe commented, joining Eva on the sidewalk.

Eva tilted her head. "Guess we'll see her upstairs."

When they got there Fran was alone in the room with Teo. Rafe was relieved to see the other man awake and alert, speaking to his guest. His complexion was much deeper than it had been yesterday. He looked good—healthy.

Fran on the other hand appeared something of a mess. Her face was streaked with tears. Purple blotches colored the area under her eyes. She'd clearly been crying for a good long time. Ironically, it looked like Teo was the one comforting her rather than the other way around. Interesting.

Eva rushed into the room, then gave her brother a big hug, squeezing him around the neck. "You're awake!"

"Hey, take it easy, sis," Teo immediately complained, though there was no real ire in his tone. "You really don't need to hug me in a viselike grip."

Eva tilted her head up in Rafe's and Fran's direction, not letting go of her brother even the slightest. "Could I have a moment alone with my muleheaded brother?" she asked them both.

Fran immediately stepped to the door, but not before giving Teo's hand another squeeze. Rafe followed her out of the room.

Rafe didn't mean to eavesdrop; he really didn't. But he couldn't help but hear the first snippet of their conversation as he was just outside the door.

"I know why you did this, Teo," Eva said. "I love you for it. But I really wish you hadn't."

Rafe heard Teo answer after a loud sigh. "I was the one who introduced you to him, Ev. I had to try and do something."

Out of respect, Rafe shut the door quietly behind him.

"You okay?" Rafe asked Fran when they were in the hallway alone together.

She nodded with a soft sniffle. "I was just so worried when I heard the news."

At least as worried as Teo's blood kin, it appeared.

Fran gave him a warm smile through trembling lips. "I'm really glad you were here for her through this."

"Me too," he simply responded.

CHAPTER FOURTEEN

Two Weeks Later

RAFE READ THE email in his inbox and couldn't help but pump a fist in the air in celebration. Paolo Bertrand had finally written to say they were anxious to sign on with Gato Rums as their sole distributor. Eva was copied in the message. Had she seen it yet?

Rising from his desk chair, he decided to find out. There was another email he'd received that he also was eager to tell her about. This one hadn't included her in the reply as he'd initiated the exchange without her knowledge. It was an exchange with one Bahamian Veterinary Center in Nassau. He couldn't wait to see her face when he told her about that one.

The sound of feminine voices echoed from the kitchen. He made his way in that direction to find her there with Nana. Both of them stood at the stove, their backs to the doorway.

Nana was stirring something on the range and not for the first time, Rafe was struck by how comforting and homely it felt to share his residence with others. He'd lived alone most of his life, even as a child. His earliest memories involved sitting on the couch watching TV by himself while his mother went to work. He'd sit that way for hours, and when she finally came home, she'd often go straight to bed. By contrast, this was a completely new experience— one that made waking up in the morning just a bit brighter.

"My brother is too clueless to even suspect," Eva was saying to her grandmother in a rather mischievous tone. Neither had yet noticed his presence behind them.

"Ay, Dios," Nana replied. "How can Teo not see how often she visits him? With all those trays of munchies she prepares and brings for him."

Some harmless gossip, then. Rafe knew they had to be speaking about Fran.

"Especially when she hears his pretty rehabilitation nurse has come by for the day," Eva added with a small giggle. They'd all agreed that it would be best for Teo to move into his old room on the first floor while his leg healed. A physiotherapist was to make biweekly house calls for his treatment. She'd started last week.

Rafe was about to announce his arrival when the door leading to the patio opened and Señor Gato wheeled his son into the kitchen in his wheelchair, his leg propped up on an extension. Without meaning to, Rafe stepped off to the side behind the wall. He wasn't even sure why, but he wasn't ready to be seen by the four of them just yet.

"What are you two so giddy about?" Teo asked the two women.

"Nada," Nana answered. "Here, taste this." She held a wooden spoon covered in a thick burgundy sauce to his mouth.

Rafe's heart pounded in his chest at the scene.

Who was he kidding? It was laughable that for a minute back there he'd actually thought he could be part of such a cozy scenario. His name may be on the deed, but this wasn't his house. Nor his land. Nor his business.

He'd acquired it all by a sheer stroke of luck. And through the sheer misfortune of the people he stood watching right now—honest, decent people who loved each other and cared enough for one another that one had literally risked his life for another.

Rafe had no right.

It became so clear in that moment what he had to do. He wanted to kick himself for not seeing the truth sooner when it was so clear in front of his nose. Rafe had no part in the picture he was looking at. He didn't belong here.

There would be no need to tell Eva about that second email, after all.

"You wanted to see me?"

Eva stepped into his study about twenty minutes later, after he'd texted her. In a way, he wished she'd taken much longer to get here. But putting off this conversation wouldn't make it any easier.

He leaned back against his chair, then motioned for her to sit in the one across from the desk.

Eva's smile faltered as she did what he asked. Clearly, she'd picked up on the overall vibe of the situation. The air between them was thick with tension.

"What's the matter, Rafe? Did something go wrong with the wash? Raul hasn't said anything to me."

He held his hand up to stop her. "No. The wash is fine. There's something else I need to speak to you about."

She tilted her head. "All right. What is it? I can tell by your face that something's not right."

Rafe's mouth had gone dry. Telling her was going to be even more difficult than he would have guessed. But he had no choice.

"I got a phone call about an investment opportunity back in the States the other day," he told her. That was the absolute truth. He got those calls fairly regularly. The next part would be where he stretched the truth.

"And?" she prompted.

"And I've decided that it's too good to pass up."

She blinked at him, her face scrunching in confusion. "I don't understand. What does that mean exactly?"

"It means I'm headed back to the West Coast to oversee it personally. You'll have to take over all my duties here."

Her eyebrows lifted, confusion flooding her face. "How long do you plan on being gone?"

"I wouldn't be able to say. Several months at least. Maybe longer."

Her mouth fell open. "What?"

"I'm sorry, Eva. But I know you can handle things on your own."

"You can't be serious about this." Her expression was so tormented, Rafe almost gave in to the urge to backtrack. But he couldn't, for either of their sakes.

"I am serious. My mind is made up. I'll be leaving immediately. I've already made arrangements for movers to pack and ship my things."

Her eyes grew wide. "You're not even staying

long enough to pack yourself? I can't believe this is happening," she stammered, outrage dripping in her voice. "How could you have decided this all on your own, without so much as running it by me? What about the contracts with the resorts? What about purchasing new equipment? All that needs to be done to meet the new demand?"

"You'll have a consultant at your disposal to assist you going forward with all of that. I know just the firm. I've already called them."

"You've thought of everything, haven't you?" She cupped her hand over her mouth. Rafe itched to reach for her, to tell her was taking it all back—to just forget what he'd said. But that would simply be putting off the inevitable.

"What a fool I've been," she continued, her voice shaky. "I thought you cared. About the distillery. About this home." She gasped. "I thought you cared about me."

It took every ounce of will he had not to react to her statement. She would never know how much he cared—so much so that he'd fallen in love her. There was no denying it now.

It was why he had to leave.

She laughed in a way that held no mirth. "I can't believe it's happening again. This was just a game to you. My entire world, everything that meant anything to me, was just a business opportunity you took a chance on. And now you can just easily walk away. Like it means nothing to you."

Her words cut him like a razor blade. To make the pain stop, he cut her.

Rafe braced himself, preparing for what he was about to do. What he told her next would deliver the final blow.

He sucked in a much-needed breath before his last strike. "Eva, that's all this ever was. Just business. And it's time for me to move on."

She wondered if he would take the paintings with him—the one of the very scene she watched now, and the one with the rising phoenix.

Eva sat cross-legged on the sand and watched the slow, crashing waves of the ocean. She couldn't bring herself to stay in the house, hearing Rafe's footsteps upstairs as he packed the bags he would be bringing with him. She couldn't watch as he walked out the door with no indication of when he might be back—if ever. Hopefully, he would take the paintings eventually, or she would have to donate them. She wanted nothing in that house that reminded her of Rafael Malta.

She'd fallen for yet another man addicted to the game, one who found it so easy to walk away once that game was over.

But this felt different. The pain felt deeper, sharper. Because somewhere along the way, sometime between the walk they'd taken on this very beach and the day they'd left the Bahamas, Eva had fallen hopelessly head over heels in love with him. She hadn't even been paying attention, and couldn't even point out when exactly it had happened. More's the pity, for all she was left with now was a broken heart.

She was so entrenched in her thoughts, it took a moment for her to register that a shadow had fallen in front of her in the sand at her feet. She looked up to find Papá standing over her.

"Nana told me I could find you here," he told her, crouching to a sitting position by her side. "Not surprising," he added. "This is where you'd come as a little girl when you wanted to get away from the house. Or from any of us."

"I wasn't trying to get away, Papá. I just needed some time alone to think."

He nodded. "Rafe stopped by to see me," he told her. "Said he'd be gone for a while. Wasn't sure when he'd be back. Does your need for alone time have anything to do with that, maybe?"

"Is he gone?" she asked, unable to control the shaking in her voice.

"Left about an hour ago."

Eva hated herself for not being able to control the sob that escaped her mouth. How weak she must seem to this strong, proud man who'd always been a pillar of support for his children. How pathetic. "He was saying his goodbyes," she said, her voice breaking with both anguish and fury.

"You're in love with him."

Her silence was answer enough. They sat in wordless silence for several moments before her father broke the quiet.

"What did he say when you asked him to stay?" he asked.

His question unnerved her. "I didn't."

Papá turned to face her. "Until very recently, you always fought for what you wanted. What happened?"

She opened her mouth, then closed it again, unsure how to answer. Papá had to be able to guess the answer to his question. After her divorce, she didn't know what warranted a fight anymore. With Rafe, she'd thought maybe her ruinous marriage was finally something she might be able to put behind her…only to have Rafe turn his back on her as well.

"You let him leave without saying anything about how you feel," he supplied at her silence.

"I was too hurt to tell him anything," she said, her heart shattering in her chest. "What good would it have done? He wanted to leave.

He didn't even want to stick around for the time it would take to do his own packing."

Her father wrapped an arm around her shoulders and pulled her tight up against his side. She leaned into him without a second thought.

"I'm sorry, *mi hija*. You should tell him when he comes back."

If he ever did. Eva had no faith that would happen. Chances were she'd never see him again, just his name on distillery business paperwork or assigned to various emails, moments she would have to lick her wounds at the reminders that came her way.

Her father continued, "In the meantime, you'll be plenty busy running a growing distillery on your own."

Eva blinked up at him in confusion. "What do you mean? Where will you be?"

"I was planning to do some traveling after the sale, remember? Now that Teo's on the mend, I think I'll resume that plan."

Eva didn't understand Papá's reasoning. Didn't he realize that everything had changed? They were back in charge. The buyer was gone. He'd left them to their own devices. "We have the distillery to run," she reminded him.

"Ah, that you will be running on your own with those consultants Rafe mentioned. You know the business like the back of your hand."

She was having trouble processing all the new information. But one thing was becoming increasingly clear to her as she listened to what her father was saying. "You really don't want to."

Papá released a deep sigh. "Did it ever occur to you that I would have fought harder to keep the distillery if I felt strongly about still running it?"

Eva could only blink at him in confusion. "I was ready to give it up a while ago," he continued to explain. "I was tired, Eva. So very tired." His chest rose and fell. "Even with Nana's help, raising two teenagers on my own drained me and wore me down. On top of the business, I was ready for a rest."

Eva's head hammered at the revelation. She'd been so selfish not to see how much of a load her father had been carrying all these years. No wonder the man was weary.

Her father continued, "So when the need to sell happened, I figured it was time. The decision was made on its own."

"Huh," was all she could muster.

"And I knew you would find your own way. You always did. You always will."

Eva absorbed the shock of her father's words as the truth fully dawned on her. While she thought he'd been devastated by the loss of the business, Papá had already made plans about moving on with his future. It was both a shocking and freeing discovery.

"So where will you go next?" she asked.

He shrugged. "Not entirely sure yet. I might start in France or Italy."

"You want to go to Europe?" She would have never guessed, figured he'd want to stick to the familiar and hop the islands of the Caribbean. How wrong she'd been.

Her father flashed her a smile. "Sure. Maybe I'll start with a winery tour. I've had enough rum for this lifetime."

The disdain in his tone made her chuckle. She swiped at the moisture on her face. Eva was going to miss him. So much was changing around her, and the changes were coming at her like missiles. "That's what you want, Papá?" she asked.

He nodded once. "It is, *mi hija*. Who knows? I might even meet somebody. I've been told that even someone as old as me can find love."

Eva gripped his hand in hers. How she admired this man. She may have his DNA building her cells, but she would never be as strong and courageous as he was.

She hadn't been brave enough to tell the man she loved that she wanted him to stay with her— had never told him how she felt.

Yet another regret. This one she may never get over.

After several silent moments, her father stood to leave, bidding her goodbye. Eva couldn't let him go just yet. She stood as well, then stopped him from turning with a hand on his forearm.

"Thank you," she told him.

He tapped her nose with his finger. "For what?"

"For having faith in me still. I know I don't deserve it. And I'm sorry." Now that she'd started, she couldn't seem to stop. The words poured out of her like a gush of water from a broken dam. "I'm sorry I let you down two years ago. I'm sorry you can't be proud of me like you used—"

Papá shushed her before she could finish. "But I *am* proud of you. I've always been proud of you. I never stopped."

Eva didn't have the words that would even come close to a fitting response. So she did the only thing she could think to do. She threw her arms around his neck and hugged him with all her strength.

There was still the matter of the cat to deal with.

Rafe bit out a curse and rested his forearms on the railing of the balcony overlooking the pool. His flight back to the States wasn't for two more days. Unwisely, he'd decided to check in to La Ola, the San Juan resort that had given them their first supply contract. Now the memories of the time he and Eva had spent here together taunted him at every turn. Had it really been only a few short weeks since they'd been here? It felt like he'd lived a lifetime since then.

A lifetime in which he'd found the woman he would foolishly fall in love with. Rafe clenched his hands into tight fists. He had to forget about her and leave Puerto Rico before he did something even more reckless. The sooner the better.

As for the cat, he still had to figure something out. Rafe pulled out his cell phone and called the only person he could think of who might be able to help him.

Patty, his former assistant in Seattle, answered on the third ring. "Hello? Rafe, is that you?" She sounded breathless and distracted.

"Hi, Patty, is this a good time?"

He heard her laugh through the tiny speaker. "As good a time as any. I was just chasing my granddaughter around the yard playing tag. For a little four-year-old tyke, she can move quite fast."

He chuckled at the picture that created in his mind. "I can imagine."

"I'm so glad you called," Patty said. "It's nice

to hear from you finally." She was probably wondering exactly why he had after all this time. He'd get right to it, then.

"I was wondering if you might be interested in adopting a stray cat?" he asked her, just blurting it out as if it made any kind of sense with no context whatsoever. "Maybe for one of your grandkids?"

Patty chuckled into the phone. "A cat? How in the world did you become responsible for a pet?"

"You wouldn't believe me if I told you."

Patty laughed harder this time. "Let me run it by Frank. The kids are always asking for pets, but I don't know… It's a big responsibility when one is already babysitting a brood of little ones."

That was progress at least; he would take it. "Thank you," he told her.

"You're welcome. So tell me. How's life on the tropical paradise of Puerto Rico?" Patty asked. "Are you at the distillery right now?"

"I'm actually in San Juan at the moment. At a luxury resort."

Patty squealed. "Oh, that sounds lovely. What are you doing there?"

"Waiting for a flight back to the States. So I can look for a new home."

Patty reaction was immediate. "What? You're coming back already? But why?"

Rafe wasn't sure what came over him at her simple questions. Before he knew it, he was pouring out the entire story, leaving nothing out—from the first day he'd arrived at the hacienda, to the night in the cave, to Teo's accident and everything before, in between and after.

Afterward, he felt spent and drained—also more than a little relieved at the unexpected purge. What had come over him?

Patty remained silent for several beats, so long that Rafe wondered if he'd gone too far and shocked the poor woman speechless. Finally, she spoke. "Will you accept some motherly advice from an old woman?"

"I could use advice of any kind right now, Patty," he admitted.

"Do you remember when you first hired me all those years ago?"

"Of course," Rafe replied, though he was perplexed as to where she might be going with this. What did her employment with him have to do with the current scenario?

"I would invite you to our family picnics and barbecues."

"I remember. That was very kind of you."

"You came to a few at first. And then you

stopped. Turned down every invitation politely but firmly. Kept saying you had scheduling conflicts, even for Sunday dinners."

Rafe began to suspect where she might be headed. He'd begun getting antsy all those years ago when he'd started growing too familiar with Patty's family—and they with him. So he'd begun to avoid them. It was easier that way. He'd pulled away before he could form any kind of bond with her husband or adult sons.

Had he just done the same with Eva?

"I think I know the point you're trying to make, Patty."

"Good," Patty said gently. "I'm glad to hear it. And there's another thing you should know."

"What's that?"

"I've never heard you speak about anyone or anything with as much emotion as you just did about this Eva."

"Thank you, Patty," he said with genuine gratitude.

"You're welcome, son." Rafe stilled; she'd never called him that before. Rafe thought of all the years of affection he might have had in his life if he'd continued to accept those invites. Such a wasted chance at some small amount of happiness in his life.

He'd simply thrown it away.

* * *

The penalty fees the airline charged him each time he changed his flight were beginning to add up, but Rafe couldn't seem to bring himself to take a car to the airport and finally fly back the West Coast.

He felt unsettled and disoriented, unable to decide which direction to move in. He was stuck. The predicament marked the first time in his life he'd ever felt indecisive about anything. It was an uncomfortable and unfamiliar feeling.

He'd been at La Ola for ten days now, getting tired of staring at the same balcony view and listening to the same sounds. It all brought back memories of the day he and Eva had spent here together.

Yet he couldn't bring himself to leave. To be more accurate, he couldn't bring himself to leave Puerto Rico. And he had nowhere else on the island to go.

Biting out a curse, her strode off the balcony, through the suite and took the elevator to the ground floor. Only one stool at the poolside bar remained empty. Rafe sat and ordered the day's lunch special.

The couple next to him were draped all over each other. Rafe had to look away, unable to watch the intimacy they shared. The shiny gold bands on their fingers looked brand-new. Finally, the woman pulled away and told her husband she'd be waiting for him upstairs.

The man reached for his bill on the counter but Rafe took it first. "It's on me."

The gentleman turned to him in surprise. "You don't have to do that, man."

"Consider it a wedding gift."

"Wow. Very nice of you." A sheepish grin spread over the man's lips. "Is it that obvious?"

He had no idea. "Very. Congratulations."

"Thanks. We're on our honeymoon."

Rafe guessed as much.

"Got married last week," he added.

"Congratulations," Rafe repeated, unable to come up with anything else to say.

"Thanks, man." He reached out and shook Rafe's hand. "And thanks for lunch. I'm Manny."

"Rafe."

"It almost didn't happen," Manny announced with zero context, though Rafe figured he could guess what he meant.

"I got cold feet," Manny explained. "I almost backed out—called off the wedding a month before the big day."

Now his interest was piqued. Manny and his wife had looked so completely in love; it was hard to believe they'd almost not gotten married at all.

"It was the most miserable time of my life," Manny said, shaking his head sadly.

"What happened?"

"I came to my senses. Realized I was just scared and anxious. But I was more scared to be without her."

"Huh."

"Luckily, she still wanted me." Manny blew out a large sigh. "To think, I almost messed it all up."

With that, the other man stood and made his way across the pool deck.

Rafe watched him walk away and felt a loosening of the tightness in his chest he hadn't even been aware had been there.

More scared to be without her.

Rafe swore out loud, earning a quizzical look from the bartender. He'd been such a fool. A stubborn and clueless fool, too afraid to take an emotional risk in case it all ended up going up in flames—like so many other times in his life.

But Eva was worth the risk.

Rafe pinched the bridge of his nose. He'd been so blind to what was so clear in front of his face. He loved Eva Gato. He needed to tell her so.

Ignoring his lunch, he pushed off the stool to

gather his things from upstairs and check out of this hotel once and for all.

His phone vibrated in his pocket with an incoming call when he reached the elevator. Rafe answered when he saw the contact name on the screen. "Hi, Patty."

"Hey, Rafe. Wanted to get back to you about the cat."

It took a moment for Rafe to process what she'd said. His mind was racing. Now that he knew what he wanted to do, he couldn't wait to set the plan in motion.

Then he remembered he'd asked Patty if she might be interested in adopting the stray feline still being housed at the veterinary center. "Yes?" he answered.

"I talked to Frank and he thinks our grandkids might be too young for a pet right now, to be honest."

"That's okay. Finding an adopter won't be necessary after all," he told her. "I think I just figured out what to do with her."

"What's that?" Patty wanted to know.

"What I should have done all along before I foolishly chickened out," he replied. "I'm going to bring her where she belongs."

It was where he belonged as well. If he was still welcome.

* * *

Eva had to read the text twice.

Her pulse had jumped when she'd first gotten the alert to see Rafe's contact icon pop up as the sender. He was texting her, a full two weeks after he'd left. A bloom of hope blossomed in her chest before she clicked to read the message.

Then her heart shattered to discover he was only sending her on a business errand. Eva tossed the cell phone onto the desk with such force it popped out of its protective case. She was an idiot to think Rafe might contact her about anything but the distillery. He was gone, probably texting her from Seattle or California—wherever his latest business venture had taken him.

He hadn't even bothered to tell her the specifics.

She took a fortifying breath and read his message once more. Apparently, a signature was needed on some document at the San Juan hotel before they could begin the exclusive distribution.

Funny, she'd thought they'd crossed every *t* and dotted every *i* that day before they'd left.

Not so, according to Rafe's text. The manager needed her there that afternoon to take care of it.

As much as she wanted to ignore the directive, Rafe was still technically her boss. She would have to go. Best to just get it over with. With a resigned sigh, Eva pulled a casual business suit of her closet. This would be the first face-to-face business meeting she'd be attending on her own, without her father or Rafe.

Another milestone for both her and the distillery, which had won yet another deal without so much as a visit to the latest resort to sign Gato as sole distributor. But she had no desire to celebrate. She felt nothing but hollow inside. The emptiness felt even worse than what she'd experienced after her divorce. Back then, she'd had the intensity of her anger at Victor to hold on to. With Rafe's absence, she had nothing.

Just a gnawing gap in the pit of her soul she didn't think would ever fill.

A little over an hour later, she walked through the lobby of the resort and made her way to the room number she'd been given. She'd had to give up her whole afternoon to sign a lousy piece of paper. What had Rafe been thinking?

That was just it. She couldn't guess the answer to that question. She'd never really known Rafe at all, it appeared.

Walking farther down the hall, she blinked

in confusion. Something was wrong. The room number she'd been given didn't lead to any kind of office or conference room. Instead, she found herself in front of a glass door that led to an outdoor patio. She walked onto the brick walkway, the scent of roses and tropical flowers pleasantly hanging in the air. This couldn't be where she was supposed to be to sign a document. On top of everything else, Rafe seemed to have sent her on a wild-goose chase.

A voice called out her name—a voice she recognized. Eva gave her head a brisk shake. She had to stop thinking about him. Now she was hearing his voice in her head.

But she heard her name again just as a familiar figure stepped out from behind a tall Flamboyant tree.

Eva's heart stopped. Was she seeing *and* hearing things?

"Rafe?"

"Hello, sweetheart."

It wasn't her imagination. He was really here. Something black-and-white and furry wiggled in his arms.

Her feet somehow worked enough to move over to where he stood. "Oh, my… Is that…?"

He held the furball up to her. "It is. I flew to get her yesterday."

"Oh, Rafe."

"I've given her a name," he said. "But we can change it if you don't like it."

Her mind was still trying to process exactly what was happening. For now, she decided to focus on the small animal she'd grown so attached to all those days ago. "What name?" she asked.

"Coqui."

Eva laughed, his answer catapulting her back in time to the day they'd visited the rain forest.

He held the cat out and Eva gingerly took her, then snuggled her face into the soft fur on its back. "I've missed her so much. I love the name you've given her."

Rafe remained silent for several moments. Then he said the words that had her pulse skittering. "And I love you," he told her. Eva's breath caught in her throat. She felt dizzy. Was this really happening?

"You do?"

Rafe nodded. "With every bit of my heart and my soul."

This had to be some kind of dream. She couldn't really be here. Rafe wasn't really saying such words to her.

"I'm so sorry, sweetheart," he told her above

her head. "For being a blind fool. I should have never left."

If this was indeed a dream, Eva wanted to remain immersed in it forever. But a cry of caution echoed in her head. There were questions that still needed to be answered, with zero doubt on Rafe's part.

"Why *did* you leave?" she asked. "And how can I be sure it won't happen again?" Eva choked back a sob as she asked the question. The thought of this happiness being yanked out of her hands yet again was enough to crush her soul. She didn't think she would survive the blow twice in one lifetime.

"Because I was skittish and scared and—" He stopped abruptly, then rubbed his forehead. "Because I didn't think I deserved you. But I vow to spend my days striving to be the kind of man who does."

Eva could only stare at him, breathless for several pauses. Finally, she found her voice. "There's nothing you need to strive for, Rafe Malta. You're the man I love. That's all I need."

His eyes darkened with emotion at her words. "Does that mean you forgive me?"

"Yes. I forgive you," she replied, with no hesitation and no qualms whatsoever.

His shoulders sagged with relief at her answer. "It's more than I deserve."

She stepped closer into his length, close enough to feel his heartbeat against her chest. "Then you'll just have to make it up to me."

Rafe pulled her in for a deep, hungry kiss that had her weak in the knees. "I know just how to start," he said against her lips.

EPILOGUE

Eva HAD TO laugh at the scene before her when she entered the kitchen. How could he still be having so much trouble operating the coffee machine after all this time? A full year and Rafe couldn't seem to master exactly which buttons to push to get the beverage exactly the way he wanted it.

Eva bumped him aside to do it herself. Before she got a chance, he grabbed her by the waist and turned her to face him for a good-morning kiss. Heaven help her—even after all this time, the man's lips against hers still melted her heart.

And the things he did to her at night had her melting all over.

She was tempted to pull him back upstairs at that thought, but they had work to do. "Good morning."

"It is now," Rafe answered with a mischievous smile.

She rubbed her gloss off his lips with her fingertips. "Go take your usual spot on the patio. I'll brew us both some coffee."

"You're an angel sent straight from heaven," he told her before turning to do as she'd said.

The statement catapulted her back in time to a little over twelve months ago, when he'd said those exact same words to her. Little had she known then just how much her life was about to change with Rafe Malta's arrival on the island. Some days she still felt the need to pinch herself to make sure all of it was real.

When she reached the table outside and sat across from him, Rafe was thumbing through his tablet. Coqui sat wrapped around his ankles, her gentle purr ringing softly through the air.

"We'll have to make a trip to the Paradiso Resort together," he informed her. "Check your calendar when you get a chance."

The statement was rather out of the blue and alarmed her. They'd been supplying the Paradiso resort exclusively since shortly after their eventful visit—when they'd been stranded on an iguana-laden island. "Is there a problem?" she asked. "Are they thinking of not re-signing us for distribution this year?"

Rafe shook his head. "No problem. I thought we might visit to celebrate. I know it's a lovely spot for a honeymoon."

Eva stilled in the act of bringing her coffee cup to her lips. Surely, she had to be hearing things. It was then she noticed the object attached to Coqui's collar—a small box with a bright red satin ribbon.

"What's that?" she asked, pointing a trembling finger at the cat.

Rafe put his tablet down and leaned over to pick up the cat, but not before she caught a sly, sneaky expression flash over his face. He held Coqui toward her.

"Open it," Rafe prompted. "It's for you."

Eva reached for the box and opened it with shaky hands, gasping when she saw what sat inside on a bed of folded satin.

A sparkling emerald cut diamond on a woven gold band. The world started to spin. Then his arms were around her, lifting her out of her seat and taking her into his embrace. She inhaled his scent deeply, reveling in the feel of him against her.

"If you don't want to go back to the Paradiso, we can go anywhere else you like. Just say yes."

Eva worked her mouth, but no words seemed to be coming forth through her lips. Like the old saying went, it appeared the cat really had gotten her tongue.

Rafe removed the ring from its box, then took her hand in his. With a steady, firm grasp he slipped it onto the finger of her left hand. Eva stared at the treasure sparkling in the sunlight, catching the myriad colors that surrounded them.

Rafe leaned in to speak into her ear. "Evalyn Gato, will you do me the honor of becoming my wife?"

Eva thought her heart might swell until it burst in her chest. She answered Rafe's question by pulling his head down to hers and kissing him with all the passion and love for him rushing through her veins.

They were both gasping for air by the time they pulled apart.

"Is that a yes?" Rafe asked, flashing her a teasing smile.

"It is, my love," she answered, unable to resist planting another kiss on his lips. "It's a yes!"

From the corner of her eye, Eva could have sworn she saw the bright green feathers of a rare parrot fly from atop a tree toward the bright blue sky.

* * * * *

If you enjoyed this story, check out these other great reads from Nina Singh

Wearing His Ring till Christmas
Whisked into the Billionaire's World
Around the World with the Millionaire
From Wedding Fling to Baby Surprise

All available now!

The atmosphere suddenly grew thick and heated.

Eva's pulse quickened, a flush crept up her cheeks. What exactly was Rafe saying? That he lay awake in his bed, remembering the two of them frolicking in the water? Heaven help her, the images she was assaulted with nearly had her rushing out of her chair to see if he might take her in his embrace the way he had yesterday on that stairwell. It had taken all the will she had then not to try to kiss him. It was taking even more now to stay still where she sat.

How much longer could they ignore what was clearly present between them? Eva knew the attraction wasn't one-sided. She could see it in the heat that swam in Rafe's eyes even now as he looked at her across the kitchen. She wasn't imagining it. Rafe wanted to kiss her, too.

Dear Reader,

Welcome to the sunny, gorgeous island of Puerto Rico. Evalyn Gato was born and grew up there. The rum distillery her family has run for generations is part of her DNA. But a soul-crushing betrayal has led to the devastating loss of the property and business. Eva and her family have no choice but to sell.

Enter Rafe Malta. Rafe is looking to rebuild his life after one too many of life's blows. He may be successful as a businessman, but through the years, he's been dealt one crushing defeat after another. Finally, it becomes too much and Rafe decides to leave his old life behind for a new start. What better way than to buy a rum distillery on a peaceful island?

Together, Eva and Rafe help each other learn to overcome the past and embrace a brand-new future. Along the way, they find true love.

I felt so fortunate to be able to write Eva and Rafe's story, one of redemption and self-forgiveness. I hope you enjoy their journey.

Nina Singh